AF540842

PERSONALITY AND ADJUSTMENT OF UNIVERSITY HOSTEL STUDENTS

PERSONALITY AND ADJUSTMENT OF UNIVERSITY HOSTEL STUDENTS

By

Dr. T.J. Mouni Suvarna Raju
M.A., M.Ed., Ph.D. (Psychology)
Principal
K.P.N. College of Education
Gantyada, Vizianagaram – 535 215, A.P.

Editors

Dr. M.V.R. Raju
M.A., Ph.D. (Psychology)
Head, Department of Psychology
Andhra University
Visakhapatnam – 530 003, A.P.

Dr. B. Prasad Babu
M.A., B.Ed., M.Phil., Ph.D. (Psychology)
Rehabilitation Counsellor
Rural Rehabilitation Extension Centre for Handicapped
Thiruvallur, Chennai – 602 001, Tamil Nadu

Dr. Digumarti Bhaskara Rao
M.Sc., M.A., M.A., M.Ed., Ph.D.
Reader & Research Director
R.V.R. College of Education
Guntur – 522 006, A.P.
digumartibhaskararao@rediffmail.com

D P H

DISCOVERY PUBLISHING HOUSE PVT. LTD.
NEW DELHI-110 002

First Published-2009

ISBN 978-81-8356-424-3

Published by:

DISCOVERY PUBLISHING HOUSE PVT. LTD.
4831/24, Ansari Road, Prahlad Street
Darya Ganj, New Delhi-110002 (India)
Phone: 23279245 • Fax: 91-11-23253475
E-mail: dphbooks@rediffmail.com
dphtemp@indiatimes.com
web: www.discoverypublishinghouse.com

Printed at:

Sachin Printers
Delhi

dedicated
to honourable dignitaries

Prof. Y.R. Haragopal Reddy
Hon'ble Vice Chancellor
Acharya Nagarjuna University
Nagarjuna Nagar, Guntur District
Andhra Pradesh

Prof. M.K. Durga Prasad
Hon'ble Vice Chancellor
Krishna University
Machilipatnam, Krishna district
Andhra Pradesh

in recognition of their
excellent services to education

Preface

Hostels in educational institutions are provided to those students who are unable to attend to the institution on time due to several reasons like distance, transport facilities, parents' support in education at home, conducive facilities available at the house, student's attitude, etc. Now-a-days, many parents, understanding the importance of education, prefer to admit their wards in hostels to make them imbibe in educational programmes without any household activities. With the academic environment available in hostel, the students try to excel in every educational activity. Of course, there are certain limitations also with the hostels. But, the advantages of the hostels outnumber their limitations. Hence, students are joining good hostels to get quality education through better academic environment.

The present study identifies that better personality adjustment leads to better hostel adjustment of students. The better personality adjustment of hostel students leads to better academic, emotional and social adjustments.

This book will be of use to psychologists and counsellors of pregnant women in attending to their roles suitably. This book will be useful to special educators and teachers also to perform their functions appropriately.

Dr. D. Bhaskara Rao

Sri Sai Soudha
D-43, S.V.N. Colony
Guntur 522006
A.P., India

Contents

1

INTRODUCTION

INTRODUCTION

Hostels in educational institutions are provided to those students who are unable to present to the institution on time due to several reasons like distance, transport facilities, parents' support in education at home, facilities available at the house, student's attitude, etc. Now-a-days, many a parent, understanding the importance of education, prefers to admit their wards in hostels to make them imbibe in educational programmes without any household activities. With the academic environment available in hostel, the students try to excel in every educational activity. Of course, there are also certain limitations with the hostels. But, the advantages of the hostels outnumber the limitations. Hence, students are joining good hostels to get quality education.

The Personality

Self and personality refer to the characteristic ways in which we define our existence. They also refer to the ways in which our experiences are organised and show up in our behaviour. From common observation we know that different people hold different ideas about themselves. These ideas represent the self of a person.

We also know that different people behave in different ways in a given situation, but the behaviour of a particular person from one situation to another generally remains fairly stable. Such a relatively stable pattern of behaviour represents the "personality" of that person. Thus, different persons seem to possess different personalities. These personalities are reflected in the diverse behaviour of persons.

The term 'personality' often appears in our day-to-day discussion. The literal meaning of personality is derived from the Latin word persona, the mask used by actors in the Roman theatre for changing their facial make-up. After putting on the mask, audience expected the person to perform a role in a particular manner. It did not, however, mean that the person enacting the given role necessarily possessed those qualities. For a layperson, personality generally refers to the physical or external appearance of an individual. For example, when we find someone 'good-looking', we often assume that the person also has a charming personality. This notion of personality is based on superficial impressions, which may not be correct.

In psychological terms, personality refers to our characteristic ways of responding to individuals and situations. People can easily describe the way in which they respond to various situations. Certain catchwords (e.g., shy, sensitive, quiet, concerned, warm, etc.) are often used to describe personalities. These words refer to different components of personality. In this sense, personality refers to unique and relatively stable qualities that characterise an individual's behaviour across different situations over a period of time. If you watch closely, you will find that people do show variations in their behaviour. One is not always cautious or impulsive, shy or friendly.

Personality characterises individuals as they appear in most circumstances. Consistency in behaviour, thought and emotion of an individual across situations and across time periods characterises her/his personality. For example, an honest person is more likely to remain honest irrespective of time or situation. However, situational variations in behaviour do occur as they help individuals in adapting to their environmental circumstances.

In brief, personality is characterised by the following features:

1. It has both physical and psychological components;
2. Its expression in terms of behaviour is fairly unique in a given individual;
3. Its main features do not easily change with time;
4. It is dynamic in the sense that some of its features may change due to internal or external situational demands.

Thus, personality is adaptive to situations. Once we are able to characterise someone's personality, we can predict how that person will probably behave in a variety of circumstances. An understanding of personality allows us to deal with people in realistic and acceptable ways. For example, if you find a child who does not like orders, the most effective way to deal with that child will be not to give orders, but to present a set of acceptable alternatives from which the child may choose. Similarly, a child who has feelings of inferiority needs to be treated differently from a child who is self-confident. Several other terms are used to refer to behavioural characteristics of individuals.

The Adjustment

The word "adjustment" came in to popular use in psychology during the 1930s and was given strong endorsement by Lawrence Shaffer's classical book "The Psychology of adjustment" which was published in 1936. In his treatment of adjustment, Shaffer emphasised the biological adaptation of the organism to its environment as the central meaning of the term (Bell, 1962).

The term adjustment is often used as a synonym for accommodation and adaptation. Strictly speaking, the term denotes the results of equilibrium, which may be affected by either of these processes (Monroe, 1990). It is to emphasise the individual's struggle to get along or survive in his or her social and physical environment.

The concept of adjustment is as old as human race on earth. Adaptability to environmental hazards goes on increasing as the human beings proceed on the phylogenetic scale from the lower extreme to the higher extreme of life. Insects and germs, in comparison to human beings, cannot withstand the hazards of changing conditions in the environment.

Man, among the living beings, has the highest capacity to adapt to new situations. Man as a social animal not only adapts to physical demands but also adjusts to social pressures.

Biologists used the term adaptation strictly for physical demands of the environment but psychologists use the term adjustment for varying conditions of social or inter-personal relations in the society. Thus, adjustment means reaction to the demands and pressure of social environment imposed upon the individual. The demand may be external or internal to which the individual has to react. Chauhan (1979) and Vonhaller (1990) explained adjustment as 'psychological survival' in much the same way as the biologist used the term adaptation to describe 'physiological survival'.

"Life presents a continuous chain of struggle for existence and survival" says Darwin. The observation was apt since every one strives for the satisfaction of their needs. In struggling to achieve something, if one finds that results are not satisfactory, one either changes one's goal or procedure. While doing so one protects one's self from possible injury to one's ego, failure or frustration. It was shifted to more defensive position in order to face the challenge of circumstances after the initial failure. This special feature of the living organism is termed as adjustment in the view of Mangal (1989).

Every student from the beginning of the first grade until finishes college education makes a long series of adjustments between the whole unique personality and the environment. The ardent desire of each boy or girl is to become an individual person having a healthy physique, a growing intellectual ability, a greater degree of emotional poise, an increased participation in social groups and such other characteristics enhance personality.

Occasionally in the use of the term 'adjustment', the implication that the most desirable state of adjustment is one in which the individual is perfectly happy and satisfied with all aspects of life and one in which had reached the level in all contacts with environment, that would be glad to persist throughout life. The best integrated and adjusted individuals would have established some reasonable goals in line with their interests, abilities and settled down to work towards those goals seriously and steadily, without unusual tensions. This implicated that adjustment means harmony between the individual and the environment.

Meaning of Adjustment

Many psychologists, sociologists, biologists and environmentalists defined adjustment. Some of the related definitions are presented in this section. The psychologists give most of the definitions.

As per Good (1945), "Psychological adjustment is the process of finding modes of behaviour suitable to the environment or to change in the environment. Biologically as a change or acquired characteristics in an organism, that enables it to meet the requirements of its environment."

Shaffer (1952) defined adjustment as 'tension reduction' mechanism.

According to Shaffer and Shoben (1956) "Life consists of a series of such sequences in which needs are aroused and satisfied. This family pattern is the process of adjustment".

Shaffer (1956) defined the relationship, which becomes established among the biological heritage or organism, the environment, and the personality is adjustment.

Lindgren (1959) defined adjustment as the act or process of establishing a satisfactory psychological relationship between the individual and his environment.

Smith (1961) defined a good adjustment as one, which is both realistic and satisfying. At least in the long run, it reduces to a minimum the frustrations, the tensions and anxieties, which a person must endure.

Shaffer (1961) defined adjustment as the process by which a living organism maintains a balance between its needs and the circumstances that influence the satisfaction of these needs.

Bhatia (1965) defined adjustment as an all-inclusive term meaning relationship between an individual and his environment through which his needs are satisfied in accordance with social demands.

Gorlow (1968) defined adjustment as the co-ordination of the individual needs and goal seeking behaviour into smoothly functioning interaction with the environment.

Bhatnagar (1968) says that adjustment refers to harmonious relationships between the individual and environment, whereas social integration enhances efficiency, co-ordination, co-operation and communication.

Coleman (1969) defined adjustment as the outcome of the individual's efforts to deal with stress and meet his needs.

Gates and Jersild (1973) defined adjustment as a continual process by which a person varies his behaviour to produce a more harmonious relationship between himself and his environment.

Eysenck (1975) defined adjustment as a state in which the needs of the individual on one hand and claims of society on the other hand are fully satisfied.

In a general way, personal adjustment is the process by which an individual applies his resources to fulfill his personal needs and maintaining harmony with the environment.

Different psychologists have defined adjustment differently but the investigator has taken the meaning of adjustment as "the degree of harmonious relationship being maintained in striking a balance between one's requirements and the varying situations in a hostel".

Process of Adjustment

Human adjustment is a never-ending process (Ruch, 1970). It starts right from the birth of the child and continues till his death. It does not stop at any time rather it goes on with life.

The adjustment process is a universal sequence that can be identified in the behaviour of organism from the lowest species up to man. Boring (1948) says that if a paramecium (single cell animal) meets an obstruction while swimming, it will backup, turn through a small angle and swim forward again.

Ray (1992) stated that the question of adjustment arises when there are certain demands or requirements that must be met or when one is confronted with problems and conflicts in various fields of life. Those must be resolved in some way or other. One creates a world of interpersonal relations and satisfactions that contribute to the continuous growth of personality. Human behaviour takes its character from the personality, which it expresses.

Odera (1995) concluded that the psychological stress might be created in an individual during the process of learning how to cope with a novel situation, the learning of new responses, skills and acquisition of new information, and aid in coping with a new environment. However, the adaptation to unfamiliar situation should be taken as a special case of responding to an alien environment.

Kulshrestha (1979) explained that adjustment is the outcome of individual efforts to deal with stress and meets his needs and the adjustment process is away in which the individual attempts to deal with stress, tensions, conflicts etc., and meet his needs. In this process the individual also makes efforts to maintain harmonious relationships with the environment.

Lazarus (1976) stated that adjustment consists of the psychological processes by means of which the individual manages to cope with various demands or pressures. Thus, adjustment is concerned with values. One cannot think of adjustment without being sensitive to the good and the bad or to the right and the wrong. Adjustment is that which brings to a person and to his social group the good and protects him from the bad.

Adjustment is a process by which a living organism maintains balance between its needs and the circumstances, which influence the satisfaction of these needs. It is therefore, a state of harmony between the needs, activities, resources of a person and the condition of his milieu (Boring, 1948). An individual not only adapts biologically to different kinds of physical demands and pressures, but also needs to adjust psychologically and emotionally, as he has to live and lead the life in interdependence with other individuals throughout his life.

Adjustment as Relatedness

Adjustment is a personal matter. Every individual makes a unique adjustment, and every individual has unique ways of adjusting. No two people have exactly the same experiences in life, nor do they have exactly the same capacities for meeting their experiences. Getzels (1975) states that no two individuals are alike even when they presumably performing the same role. Each individual stamps the role with the characteristic style of his own personality.

An individual has been adjusted simply because he is alive. The outer forces acted on him, required him to change and deal with whatever capacities were available to him. These forces originate in his biological needs, other people and his cultural milieu.

Life is a continuous interplay of such forces many of which are created by the individuals and many of which are not, but regardless of their sources they demand responses from the environment (Coe, 1972).

Adjustment in Social Aspect

In adjustment the two crucial factors were the individual and the environment. In the study of the individual, the considerations were the heredity and biological factors, the psychological factors and the quality of socialisation given to him, whereas, the environment includes all the social factors.

Adler's (1930) view that social interest may be regarded as one of the important determinants of adjustment because the individual has to adjust in a social situation.

How far one is adjusted can be ascertained by one's social development and adaptability to the social environment. Social adjustment requires the development of social qualities and virtues in an individual. It also requires that one should be social enough to live in harmony with his social beings and feel responsibility and obligations towards his fellow beings, society and country (Prasad, 1993).

A significant aspect of psychological adjustment is adjustment with other people. In popular usage, it is likely to regard a person as a well-adjusted person who 'gets along' with other people. Such a person may be pleasant, considerate, likable and socially deft.

In simple words, adjustment is an all-inclusive term meaning relationship between an individual and his environment through which his needs are satisfied in accordance with social demands. A person is said to adjust, when he is so related to reasonably adequate environment that he is relatively happy, efficient and has a certain degree of social feeling.

Dandekar (1981) stated that a well-adjusted person always accepts his own limitations. He does not blame others for his deficiencies. He does not run away from challenging situations. When he meets with a conflict he tries to resolve it on sound basis. Tallent (1978) says that, well-adjusted people are regarded as successful in the art of living.

Healthy Personality as Adjustment

A number of theorists have chosen to emphasise the function of personality in mediating the adjustment of the individual. Personality consists of the varied and yet typical efforts at adjustment that are carried out by the individual (Hall, 1978). One of the major contemporary views of personality is that it is molded by the individual's efforts to meet the demands of daily living. Thus, a personality is considered to be maladjusted when the individual is unable to adapt to the requirements of the social group of which he is a member. In short, the sum of the individual's movements as he adapts himself to the environment is personality. Instead of being a thing in itself, personality becomes a consensus of what can be observed about the actions of a human being.

Thorpe (1965) stated that psychologists who favour the adjustment view consider the data of personality to be valid only to the extent that they emerge from behaviour itself.

O'Connell (1974) stated that the term personality, in seventy years ago was regarded as mental health. The concept of an average person can be treated if he adjusts to the society. In recent times also, some psychologists defined healthy personality as adjustment. According to Eysenck's (1978) personality is more or less stable and enduring organisation of a person's character, temperament, intellect and physique, which determines his unique adjustment to his environment.

Allport (1961) defined personality as the dynamic organisation with in the individual of those psychophysical systems that determine his unique adjustment to the environment.

Human beings constantly strive toward goals, which gratify their biological and psychological needs. Sometimes people reach their goals with relative ease but when their needs are frustrated, i.e., unsatisfied needs, and causes maladjustment in the person. The unsatisfied physical needs are generated by deficits in the organic structure and chemical balance of the body, the psychological and social needs are both natural drives and urges are learned. Both types of needs create tension in the individual, which leads to action (goal seeking). When an individual is blocked in reaching a goal, he may seek to reach the goal with renewed vigour, adopt a substitute goal (signs of a realistic and well adjusted person), try to reach the original goal by devious means (signs of being an unrealistic and offensive person) or withdraw into a world of fantasy (indicating maladjustment).

Human adjustment is thus, a never-ending process of dealing with frustration. The adjusted personality is the normal representation of needs while the exaggerations lead to maladjustment. The adjusted personality is one, which bears a realistic relation to physical and social facts. In simple words, well-adjusted people tend to have a reasonably accurate evaluation of themselves in relation to their world and hence have a fairly realistic level of aspiration. Maladjusted people on the other hand, tend to be unrealistic to set their aspirations either too high or too low leading to inevitable failure (Sharma, 1972).

Hostel Environment Adjustment

This refers to the degree of harmonious relationship being maintained in striking a balance between one's requirements and the varying situations in a hostel.

Takahashi and Majima (1994) investigated the framework of social relationships that affect adjustment to the transition from home to the college campus dormitory. They concluded that the same age dominant type students easily developed the social relationships with new age mates. This study indicates that the individual factor like age, affects the social adjustment in hostel students.

In another study Barthelemy and Fine (1995), attempted to identify residence hall factors that enhance adjustment to college. They concluded that, for both men and women personal support and group cohesiveness were positively correlated with most adjustment dimensions. Also for women, group cohesiveness was positively related to academic adjustment and personal-emotional adjustment. For men, personal support and order were positively correlated with academic adjustment.

Thus, the studies clarified that the better adjustment in hostels leads to better academic achievement, better personal-emotional adjustment and better group relations.

The term 'hostel' refers to the place of residence for psychopathic patients in western context in one sense they used the terms like 'student resident halls', 'college campus dormitories', etc., whereas in Indian context, the term 'student hostels' denotes just like student residence halls or college campus dormitories.

NEED FOR THE STUDY

Several studies have been reported in the area of social, educational, health and emotional adjustment of campus students of both sexes. Some studies try to relate adjustment with variables like intelligence, achievement, age, sex, socio-economic status, needs, anxiety and security. Student reaction to frustration has also been studied. A few studies focussed on the nature, causes and extent of indiscipline among students. The relation between indiscipline and variables like achievement, participation in co-curricular activities etc., were also examined.

Although university departments of psychology have undertaken quite a few studies in the area of adjustment, much still remains to be done (Mitra, 1972).

In India about 80 per cent of the people live in rural areas. Obviously, the students from rural areas will have to get into hostels when they pursue academic courses (Arts, Science, Medical, Engineering and Law) the colleges for which are mostly located in district headquarters.

Krishnan (1992) stated that the students who have completed their higher secondary or graduate education either in their own native places or in very nearby towns are constrained to move towards cities, where they have to face new environmental situations. Also, the hostel students of all academic and professional courses constitute a group of heterogeneity and complexity, which is due to the variations prevalent among them in terms of region, locality, custom, language, style, caste, religion etc. It is in this context, the establishment of harmonious relationship with peer-groups assumes importance. The peer-group relationship is highly dependent on the adjustment of these students in their residence.

A review of the studies carried out in the field of adjustment as reported in the three surveys of Educational research edited by Buch (1991) reveals that no systematic attempt has yet been made to develop a tool for the assessment of hostel adjustment of professional course entrants.

Bridges (1991) mentioned in psychological reports that the direct adjustment studies are reducing in West, with a similar title and with other psychological factors, the studies are in progress. Whereas in India, the adjustment studies are very limited and a lot of work on adjustment is to be done. Concerned to hostel student adjustments, the works are more in western context and those works are limited in India. There is a necessity to conduct more studies on student adjustments and environmental adjustments in hostel.

The researcher felt that there is a need to conduct a study on hostel students based on adjustment with personality and environmental factors. The researcher selected some suitable individual variables to study on personality and environmental adjustments on hostel students to know the comparison of different independent variables across the different individual factors.

More specifically, the research aims to examine the comparative adjustments of the hostel students based on their age, sex, nationality, permanent place of residence, faculty, previous and present hostel experiences, and economic status of the students.

Students of 25 years and above shows one type adjustment and certainly it would differ with that of the students below 25 years of age. Age acts as an important demographic variable in the student community. In the same way gender also acts as an important dependent variable in student adjustments. Girl students adjustments are differ from the boys.

In Andhra University some foreign students are also studying in the campus. It would be better if nationality variable is also included as dependent variable for comparison with the Indian students' adjustment. As discussed in the previous pages, the permanent place of residence, that is, rural or urban variable also shows the adjustments and variations particularly in our country.

Basing on the qualifications of the students, that is, faculty variable, it would be possible to understand the differences in adjustments. Previous hostel experience is also mattered as far as his behaviour is concerned, because of his exposure to more situations and students. Another important variable that is, economic status played a vital role as it is interlinked with all other variables.

The study is useful to know more about the comparison between groups in various dimensions of adjustment and also to know more about the relationships of various dimensions related to personality and hostel adjustments.

After identifying the problem for the study, the researcher gathered the information and material from various sources related to hostel environments, student adjustments, personality factors with adjustments and the relative studies, comparative studies on adjustment. All these related studies are reviewed in the next chapter.

2

REVIEW OF RESEARCH

The present study examines the relationship between personality and hostel environment adjustment of students. The term 'adjustment' was an older concept, which enhanced the number of studies. But studies exploring relationship between adjustments as influenced by personality factors are however, limited in number. In view of hostel adjustment, the studies are very limited. In the areas of adjustment with other factors like, Sociological, Psychological, Philosophical, Educational etc., there are hundreds of studies.

Some of the related studies are adopted for the literature of the present study. This chapter for convenience is categorised into two sections. Section I included studies of different nations and section II included Indian studies on personality and hostel adjustments.

STUDIES IN ABROAD

This section is subcategorised into the variables belonging to demographic, personality and hostel environmental factors.

1. Demographic Variables

The studies based on Age and Nationality was mentioned in this group of variables. Only one direct study on Sex differentiation was noted. In the Nationality, most of the studies are from Western, and very few studies were done on Asian students like Japanese and Chinese.

(i) Gender

Street and Kromrey (1994) examined the differences in adjustment issues for 171 male and 160 female adolescent students. They found female students were more likely than males to experience difficulties with self-esteem, depression and anxiety. Males were more likely to experience difficulties with substance abuse.

Number of studies done on the adjustment of sex, but clubbed with other dimensions, are mentioned and reviewed in the following dimensions.

(ii) Nationality

Furukawa and Shibayama (1993) studied to construct and discriminate function to prediction adjustment in foreign culture. It was the study of 123 Japanese adolescent students studied abroad in home stay for one year. The results declared that the Japanese students could not adjust properly in foreign culture and also suffered emotional distress. This study mentioned about the maladjustment in foreign culture, whereas in the category of adjustment studies, Tanaka, Takai, Kohyama and Fujihara (1994) studied about the adjustment patterns of international students in Japan. The sample of this study consists of 237 international students among 70.2 per cent male population in 7 national universities of Japan. Factors analysed with respect to demographic traits showed that the Asian students were less adjusted than those of Western and Latin American cultures. Those more proficient in the Japanese language did not prove to be better off. Scholarship recipients were better adjusted than those who rely on private sources for fund.

Kaczmarek, Matlock, Merta, and Ames (1994) compared the student adaptation to the college for 29 international and 57 U.S. Students. International students significantly lower on the social, institutional attachment and goal commitment. However, international students experienced a more difficult college transition than US students. They have had a more difficult time, seek appropriate assistance, as those who rated they had received significant help from a faculty member reported a significant increase in psychological and somatic complaints.

Barrat and Huba (1994) studied about the factors related to international undergraduate student adjustment in an American community. 170 international undergraduates completed a mail survey assessing motivation, self-esteem, inter-personal relationship, participation in activities, English language skills and community adjustment. In the evaluation, students showed good adjustment in English language skills with self-esteem in interpersonal relationships.

Jou and Fukada (1995) examined the effect of source of social support on adjustment, used the measures of needed support, actual support, and the disparity between the two, on 64 Chinese students in Japan. The possible sources of social support were Japanese professors, Japanese students, other foreign students and Japanese friends off – campus. The results concluded that the students who have taken help or social support from professors adjusted better than those students who have taken social support from Japanese students.

Chiu (1995) explored the influence of anticipatory fear, both on natural processes of adjustment for 39 Asian Foreign students during their first academic year in the US, and on the effectiveness of a cross-cultural orientation programme based on I.L. Janis (1985) stress inoculation treatment (SIT). Students with different levels of anticipatory fear differed in their responses to SIT, with the low-fear group showed the clear signs of benefit. Findings suggested that how a person responds to novelty and uncertainty was a key factor in cross-cultural adjustment.

Jou and Fukada (1996) investigated adjustment of Chinese students in Japan, and examined whether their adjustment differed according to their country of origin, gender, age, proficiency in the Japanese languages, or length of residence. 89 Chinese and Taiwanese postgraduates in Japan completed rating scale measures of adjustment students from Taiwan scored higher on adjustment. Male students reported higher adjustment on academic and cultural social scales. Students with a longer period of stay or higher proficiency in the Japanese language had higher scores on adjustment.

Jou and Fukada (1996b) examined the effects of personality and social support on adjustment of 33 Chinese Students in Japan. It was a longitudinal study and the responses were taken for 4 successive periods of just arrived, 3, 9, and 12 months. The results concluded that the social support was the positive predictor of adjustment.

Eassau and Trommsdorff (1996) examined whether 162 North American, 111 German and 92 Malaysian college students differed with respect to problem and emotion focussed coping styles, and studied the extent of variance within each cultural context and the relationship between physical symptoms and coping styles. Results show that in dealing with academic problems, Malaysian students used more emotion, focussed coping than other students. North American and German students with high scores and emotion, focussed coping experienced fewer symptoms; whereas the reverse relationship was found with the Malaysian group.

Furukawa (1997) conducted a study to examine whether or not the cultural distance influenced psychological adjustment of international exchange students. The study conducted on 211 Japanese students with a host of 23 countries around the world and before and after the 12-item general health questionnaire, Maudsley Personality Inventory and Cultural Distance Questionnaire were administered. The results indicated that greater the cultural distance more the psychological distress in the student community. Food played the greatest impact on the intercultural adjustment.

Abe, Talbot and Geelhoed (1998) studied the effects of a peer programme on international student adjustment. 60 newly admitted international graduate and undergraduate students, the majority of whom come from Asian countries participated in an International Peer Programme (IPP). Of these students, 28 IPP participants answered student adaptation to college questionnaire (SACQ). Scores were compared to those of 32 international students who did not participate in the peer programme. Results suggest that the

IPP participants showed significantly higher social adjustment scores than the non-participants. Additionally, students from Asian countries had more difficulty in adjusting to campus life than international students from Non-Asian countries.

On overall studies, Asian students are less adjusted in Western cultures. International students experienced more difficult college transition, as well as emotion-focussed coping.

2. Personality Variables

The personality variables adopted for this study are Self-pity, Loneliness, Emotionality, Health adjustment, Academic adjustment and Social adjustment. The literature related to these variables has been reviewed for each dimension.

(i) Self-pity

The related studies purely based on self, self-confrontation, self-feelings, self-esteem etc., were abstracted in this portion.

Rim (1989) examined about the self-confrontation and coping styles of 20 male and 20 female undergraduate students. Sex was found to be a moderating variable, with males and females' results differed. Findings resemble those from a study indicating a relationship between extraversion and neuroticism, self-confrontation and coping styles.

Tobacyk and Driggers (1989) investigated the self-monitoring as a moderator of relationships between traditional religious belief and personality adjustment. Results of a test battery administered to 211 college students suggest that low self-monitors show the strongest adaptive effects of religious belief on personality adjustment.

Aspin Wall and Taylor (1992), drawing on cognitive adaptation theory, optimism, psychological control, and self esteem were explored as longitudinal predictors of adjustment to college sample of 672 freshman. Controlling for initial positive and negative mood, the beneficial effects of optimism, control and self-esteem on adjustment were mediated by the non use of avoidance coping, greater use of active coping, and greater seeking of social support.

The results of a two-year follow-up indicated that self esteem and control predicted greater motivation and higher grades, controlling for college entrance examinations scores.

Ichiyama, Colbert, Laramore and Heim (1993) examined the relationship of self-concealment to psychosocial adjustment in 200 female and 144 male college students. They found that the self-concealment was significantly correlated with self-reported anxiety, depression, shyness and negative self-esteem. The tendency of self-conceal was also found to differently related to the adjustment variable as a function of sex.

Graziano, Jensen-Campbell and Finch (1997) examined about the self can be conceptualised as a mediating agent that translates personality into situated good-directed activities and adaptation. This research used a level of analysis approach to link personality dimensions (Level-I) to self systems (Level-II) and the teacher ratings of adjustment in African American, Mexican American and European American students in the sample of 317 students. The results concluded that adjustment factor linked up with other personality factors like personality structure, personality development and age related adoptions to social context.

Greenier, Kernis, McNamara and Waschull (1999) examined the extent to which level and stability of self-esteem predicted the impact that everyday positive and negative events had on individuals feelings about themselves 130 undergraduate participants recorded the most positive and most negative event that occurred each day Monday through Thursday for a period of two weeks. Students then indicated the extent to which they feel better or worse. The negative and positive events had a greater impact on personality factors. Self-esteem differed from one situation to other and in acceptance or rejection of social situations.

As the above studies indicated that the 'self' was an important factor in adjustment.

(ii) Loneliness

Clinton and Anderson (1999) studied about the social and emotional loneliness: gender differences and relationships with self-monitoring and perceived control. The sample consists of

50 men and 50 women. The population was African-American people. Both men and women experienced emotional loneliness with variation in the causes.

(iii) Emotionality

Gerdes and Mallickrodt (1994) studied on emotional, social and academic adjustment of 208 undergraduate college students. It was a longitudinal study of retention in the six years of duration. Results indicate that two different sets of items best discriminated among good standing students and among poor standing students. Generally emotional and social adjustment items predicted attrition as well or better than academic adjustment items.

(iv) Health Adjustment

Leong and Mallinckrodt and Kralj (1990) investigated the cross-cultural variations in stress and adjustment among 75 Asian and 129 Caucasian graduate Students. Asian students reported experiencing fewer stressful life events, fewer chronic health problems and fewer total physical health problems than did Caucasian students. There were no significant differences between the two groups, in terms of psychological health, but Asian students showed greater difficulties with memory and hallucination in relation to Caucasians greater difficulties with drug use problems.

Pennebaker Colder and Sharp (1990) conducted work on "Accelerating the coping process" on the basis of their previous work, freshmen should evidence improved health after writing about their thoughts and feeling associated with entering college. The self reports of homesickness and anxiety were taken from the 130 students. By years end, experimental subjects were either superiors or similar to control subjects in grade average and in positive moods, no effects emerged as a function of when people wrote, suggesting that the coping process can be accelerated.

Iwata (1994) conducted a study on 130 Japanese students out of which 46 male and 84 female students participated, to investigate the relationship between intolerance of waiting - stress and health, while another set of 125 students participated in a study to investigate the relationship between intolerance of waiting stress and personality. In the results, correlation coefficients between intolerance for waiting - stress and health and personality measures were low but significant. Higher intolerance for waiting-stress was linked with greater physical and psychological symptoms and with maladjusted personality.

Bernard, Hutchison, Levin and Pennington (1996) examined in three experiments, the relationship among health related constructs of ego strength, hardiness, self-esteem, self- efficacy, optimism and maladjustment in 589 college students. The results stated that there was a relationship between health and personality factors in the way of adjustment. However, healthy personality leads to healthy adjustment.

Thus the studies indicate that Asian students suffer with health problems and poor health leads to maladjusted personality.

(v) Academic Adjustment

Smith and Baker (1987) studied about 61 first year college freshmen decidedness regarding academic major and adjustment to college. They concluded that a relationship between decidedness regarding academic major and college adjustment emerged during the second semester. Adjustment problems associated with lack of academic major are discussed.

Chartrand (1990) studied about a causal analysis to predict the personal and academic adjustment of non-traditional students. The subjects in this study were 179 non-traditional undergraduate and adult special students. The results indicated that the data were consistent with the major hypotheses advanced in the model. Self-evaluation and commitment to the student role both had a direct effect on student role congruence, which in turn had a direct effect on academic performance and personal distress.

Brooks and Dubois (1995) investigated the individual and environmental predictors of academic and psychological adjustment during the first year of college in 56 students. Results showed that although individual variable (American College testing score, problem solving skills, surgency/intellect, emotional stability) were related most strongly to adjustment, environmental variables (social support, daily hassles and distance from home) made significant incremental contribution to the prediction of grade point average, social adjustment and psychological symptoms.

The studies indicate that the academic adjustment depends upon the so many other psychological factors.

(vi) Social Adjustment

The studies related to all the social aspects like peers, family, group relations, etc.

Berndt, Miller and Park (1989) examined 169 adolescents' perceptions of friends and parents influence on aspects of their school adjustment. The students perceived parents as more influential than friends. There were no significant relationships, however, between the measures of perceived influence and of student's own adjustment. Students who were better adjusted to school did not consistently report either more or less influence of friends.

Rice, Cole and Lapsley (1990) examined the relation between adolescent-Separation-individuation, family cohesion and college adjustment on large college student sample. The model specified that family cohesion; positive separation feeling and independence from parents would predict college adjustment. The results indicated that the positive separation feelings factor was a better predictor of college adjustment than independence from parents or family cohesion.

Defour and Hirsch (1990) studied about a social network approach of the adaptation of 89 black graduate students. Findings indicate that the black graduate students who were well in their academic aspect showed better adjustment and also fewer dropouts from the department.

Lapsley, Rice and FitzGerald (1990) assessed the relationship between late adolescent attachment to parents and peers and personal identity, social identity and adjustment to college, among 148 male and 105 female college students, 130 of whom were freshmen. In the results, freshmen scored higher on personal identity than did upperclassmen. Women reported less alienation from peers, had more trust and better communication with peers and had higher scores on personal identity and social identity.

Lopez (1991) examined about the patterns of family conflict and their relation to college students adjustment in 122 male and 332 female students. In the results, females and students who reported high levels of marital conflict in their current family environments evidenced lower personal college adjustment. Students academic adjustment maybe most at risk if they are conflict dependent on both parents simultaneously, while their personal adjustment maybe negatively affected by a conflict relationship with one or both parents.

Jay and D'Augelli (1991) assessed patterns of social support and adjustment to University life and a comparison of 84 African - American and 81 white freshmen. African-American students reported significantly less support available than white students, but this difference disappeared when family income was used as a covariate. African-American and white students did not differ in adequacy of social support. Even with family income and prior academic performance co-varied. African-American students grade point averages were significantly lower than white students. No differences in well-being were found.

Schweitzer, McGovern and Robbins (1991) used the utilisation focussed evaluation model, to evaluate the outcomes of an orientation seminar on early adjustment of 113 college entering freshmen, Findings support the use of a freshmen seminar as an intervention for promoting early academic and social adjustment to college life. The seminar seemed successful at increasing students' knowledge of the university providing available support services and promoting adjustment to the campus social environment.

The above same authors in 1993 investigated the interaction effects between goal instability and social support on college adjustment. The study conducted on 113 college freshmen. Results declared that students with low goal instability who perceived a high level of support had higher levels of semester end adjustment than students who perceived a low level of support. The former used the available social support, both within and outside the classroom, to more effectively adjust to the university environment. Students with moderate levels of goal instability were not affected by social support.

Robbins, Lese and Herrick (1993) investigated the interaction between social support and goal instability to predict adjustment to college life for 198 freshmen students prior to this research, Schweitzer et al., (1993) investigated the same topic in another university. In the results high-goal directed individuals showed better social adjustment.

Zakahi, Jordon and Christopher (1993) studied about the social adjustment to college: Communication apprehension and social network development among college students. The study concluded on 88 college students revealed that students with high communication apprehension (CA) adjusted more quickly to new social environment compared to low and moderate CA.

Reggio, Watring and Throckmorton (1993) examined the interrelations of the social skills inventory and various self-report measures related to the psychosocial adjustment of 136 undergraduate college students. Possession of social skills was positively correlated with perceived social support and most of the measures of psychosocial adjustment. Social skills combined with perceived social support predicted certain aspects of adjustment, particularly satisfaction with college. Students showed satisfaction with life in general, and reduced perceptions of loneliness.

The above studies revealed that the better social relationships lead to better personality adjustment

(vii) Other Related Studies on Personality Adjustment

The above-mentioned studies related to the dimensions of personality and adjustment. There were so many other supported studies on personality and adjustment on student community. The closely related studies were mentioned in this portion.

Lapsley, Rice and Shadid (1989) examined the relationship between psychological separation and adjustment to college in 130 freshmen and 123 upper classmen. Freshmen tended to show more psychological dependencies on mother and father, and poorer social and personal-emotional adjustment to college than did upperclassman. A pervasive relationship was found between separation and adjustment. Sex effects also emerged, with women showing more psychological dependencies than men.

Martin and Dixon (1989) studied the effects of freshman orientation and locus of control on adjustment to college on 315 freshman students. Results show that although locus of control seemed to have had an effect on students' adjustment to college, orientation attendance did not have any effect.

Kenrick, McCreath, Govern and King (1990) examined the interaction of personality dimensions like adjustment, likeability, self-control, social inclination, intelligence, dominance and taxonomy of every day settings. Interactions show some setting seen to allow more expression of some traits. Main effect shows some setting seen as more generally illuminative and some traits as more generally visible.

Mooney, Sherman and Lopresto (1991) examined an internal academic locus of control, a high level of self-esteem, and a perception that the distance from home was just right were related to four dimensions of college adjustment namely personal, academic, social and attachment. The sample consists of 88 female freshmen. Regression analysis revealed that each predictor variable significantly increased the overall predictive accuracy of college adjustment. No associations were found between actual distance and the various dimensions of college adjustment.

Rice (1992) aimed to chart late adolescent individuation from freshman to junior year in college, further examined previously reported sex differences in separation-individuation and college adjustment, and assess the with in year and across- year association between individuation and adjustment. 130 students among 81 from junior year participated in this study. The results indicated significant increases in individuation from parents' overtime along most but not all dimensions of individuation for both men and women. Gender specific patterns of individuation/adjustment emerged in freshman and junior year. In general, independence from parents in freshman year did not predict junior year college adjustment.

Chartrand (1992) studied by testing a model of non-traditional student adjustment, predictors and consequences of psychological adjustment were examined. Results supported the feasibility of the model. Academic and non-college environmental variables were predictive of institutional commitment and an absence of psychological distress, which in turn predicted intended continuance in school. Implications of the results were related to the special academic and personal needs of non-traditional students.

Kenny and Donaldson (1992) studied about the relationship of parental attachment and psychological separation to the adjustment of 162 first year college women. Close and positive attachments were normative and adaptive to student's levels of functional and emotional separations were not related to adjustment. Most students believed that their values and attitudes were similar to their parents, and attitude similarity was associated with adjustment, conflict independence or low levels of anxiety, guilt and resentment in the parental relationship was the dimension of separation-individuation most related to adjustment.

Grant, Smith, Sinclair and Salts (1993) examined the impact of natural parent or custodial parent marital status on college adjustment and the impact of age at parental divorce on college adjustment. Sample consists of 341 freshmen, 65 of which were from divorced homes. Results indicated that marital status does not influence the adjustment of the students, whereas age at the time of parental divorce affected the student adjustment.

Holmbeck and Wandrei (1993) assessed the individual and relational predictors of adjustment in first-year college students. The sample consists of 286 students among 182 women and 104 men students. Findings revealed that the separation-individuation, family relations and personality variables were better predictors of adjustment than were the cognitive indicator or home-leaving status. Results also varied as a function of gender, less well adjusted men were more disconnected from significant others, whereas less well-adjusted woman exhibited higher levels of separation anxiety and enmeshment seeking.

Garbarino and Strange (1993) examined the family systems of 118 college-age adult children of alcoholics and the consequences of that experience for the adjustment to college during the freshman year. Family environmental aspects and parental alcohol abuse were played an important role in adjustments.

Nelson, Hughes, Handal and Katz (1993) examined whether the structural intactness of the family and/or perceived family conflict was related to young adult adjustment as assessed by measures of ego identity status and psychological distress. 285 undergraduates were classified as belonging to an intact 2-parent family or a non-intact family, and as coming from homes characterised by low, medium or high levels of conflict. Findings support the psychological-wholeness model, which posits family conflict as the critical variable affecting adjustment.

Montgomery and Haemmerlie (1993) examined the relationship between adjustment to college, drinking patterns, and various aspects of student life (e.g. Fraternity or sorority membership in 114 university students. While consumption of beer was not related to students' adaptation to college, consumption of hard liquor was related to both academic and personal-emotional adjustment. Also, belonging to a fraternity or sorority was negatively related to both academic and personal-emotional adjustment but was positively related to social adjustment and overall drinking behaviour.

Martin and Dixon (1994) investigated the impact of orientation attendance and locus of control on the adjustment of 242 traditional full time college students to college life. Results indicated that students with an internal locus of control orientation scored higher on the freshman transition questionnaire, indicating more successful adjustment to college life. No relationship was found between attendance at freshman orientation and adjustment to college.

Schultheiss, Palladine and Blustein (1994) tested the hypothesis that the conjoint variance of psychological separation and parental attachment is more strongly related to college student development and adjustment. The study conducted on 73 female and 66 male college students. For college student development there was support for the conjoint hypothesis for the women but not for the men. For college student adjustment, there was no support for the conjoint hypothesis for the women and limited support for the men.

Lecci, Okun and Karoly (1994) were examined life regrets and current goals, as predictors of psychological adjustment on 155 students. Relative to regrets, goals were perceived as more impact, important, controllable, achievable, socially supported, and desirable, and as occupying more time and energy. Further more, regrets contributed to the prediction of psychological adjustment after controlling for negative affectivity. A content analysis of respondents' regrets is presented and related to chronological age and gender.

Valentiner, Holahan and Moos (1994) investigated an integrative model of mediating and moderating mechanisms in the coping process was examined in a two year, prospective frame work with 175 college students using the single group and multi-group LISREL analysis. Results concluded that changes in adjustment had direct impact of the family support associated with psychological adjustment in coping process.

Haemmerlie, Steen, and Benedicto (1994) investigated confliction independence from parents, adjustment and alcohol use among 109 college students at a mid western technical university. Results showed that greater alcohol use was associated with having achieved less conflict independence from parents, the most frequent and strongest relationships occurred with respect to the mother student relationship. The results suggested that the parent student relationship has an impact on late adolescent development and that it also may play a role in alcohol use by college students.

Tloczynski (1994) studied the opening up meditation, college adjustment and self-actualisation. In their study, 45 subjects were divided into groups for opining up meditation, relaxation and control using scores on the anxiety scales of the college adjustment sealers. High dropouts leaving 3, 4 and 3 subjects respectively in the meditation, relaxation and control groups compromised the data analysis.

Rice and Whaley (1994) examined student parent attachment in 131 undergraduates. Students completed questionnaires about their quality of their attachment relationships and about their adaptation to college during the 3rd, 9th and 15th weeks of a semester. Attachment to both parents was consistently important for women's adjustment. For men, attachment to the father was an important predictor for adjustment only during the high distress period before the end of the semester.

Rehulkova, Blatny and Osecka (1995) studied about the adolescents coping styles: A relation to the temperament. The copying strategies are determined by extraversion and neuroticism 309 students were administered measures of coping strategy and personality. It was conducted that neuroticism was associated with coping strategies of the disengagement type, and extraversion with strategies of the engagement type.

Silverthorn and Gekoski (1995) assessed the relationship among stress from parental pressure, independence from parents, self-efficacy and adjustment to University in 963 first year undergraduates. Results showed there was a strong relationship between adjustment and social desirability along with personality factors.

Adan and Felner (1995) explored notions of ecological congruence and person environment fit by examining relationships among personal and family background characteristics and the adjustment of 188 freshmen entering either a traditionally and predominantly white college or a traditionally and predominantly black college. Results indicated that there was no relationship of inter-racial experience to white students. Black students attending predominantly white college prior to inter-racial experience was associated with better adjustment to college.

Kenny and Rice (1995) reviewed the attachment model and its relevance for understanding the psychological mechanisms available for meeting the developmental and adjustment challenges of late adolescent college students. Attachment is then discussed in the concept of life–span development, stress, coping and adjustment. Existing research supports an escalation between secure parental attachment and adjustment for first year college students.

Saklofske and Kelly (1995) examined the relationship between personality and coping strategies with 196 undergraduates among 146 women. Students completed the Eysenck personality questionnaire and the coping inventory for stressful situations. Neuroticism accounted for 37 per cent of the variance in emotion-focussed coping. Personality and gender were not substantial predictors of other coping strategies.

Ramanaiah, Byravan and ThuHien (1996) investigated the construct validity of Weinberger's six-group typology of adjustment by testing the hypothesis that the six personality types have different personality profiles. 170 Psychology undergraduates among 84 men and 86 men students completed the Weinberger adjustment inventory and the revised NEO personality inventory. Results strongly supported the tested hypothesis.

Protinsky and Gilkey (1996) collected random samples of 102 women students from a small private college were assessed concerning their levels of individuation, intimacy, intimidation, parental triangulation and personal authority. These concepts formed the construct of personal authority and were tested as to their relationship to self-esteem, physical health and college adjustment. Results generally supported better adjustment for those women who had higher levels of personal authority.

Damji, Clement and Noels (1996) examined the effect of situational variations of identity and their relationship to measure of psychosocial adjustment. Sample consists of 295 native Anglophone students. Results indicated that an exclusively Anglophone identity was related to a higher level depression, lower self-esteem and a higher level of stress than the other modes of acculturation, but only when the variability in identity with the English group was high students who were committed to English identity experienced more psychological adjustment problems.

Weiss and Schwarz (1996) examined Baumrinds T3 conceptual framework using a multiple informant design and an older adolescent population with 178 college students and their families as participants the present study found many of the predicted relations between parent child-rearing style (Authoritative, Democratic, Non-directive and Unengaged,) and their adolescent children's behaviour in the 4 domains assessed: personality, adjustment, academic, achievement and substance use.

Halamandaris and Power (1997) investigated the relationship between the two broad personality dimensions of neuroticism and extraversion and dysfunctional attitudes, as well as the relationship between dysfunctional attitude, perceived social support, loneliness and general well-being during the transition to University life in 124 students. Results indicate dysfunctional attitudes correlate significantly with all the personality and psycho-social adjustment variables, and personality (Extraversion, Neuroticism, Self-esteem, Interpersonal trust) and dysfunctional attitudes contribute significantly to the prediction of perceived social support and psycho-social adjustment to university life.

Leong, Bonz and Zachar (1997) studied about the coping styles as predictors of college adjustment among 161 freshmen. Results show that academic adjustment and personal/emotional adjustment were related to the coping strategies, while social adjustment and attachment/goal commitment were not.

Cherian and Cherian (1998) collected the information on the adjustment problems of first year university students in developed countries, but comparatively little is known about such problems in Asia and Africa. This study of a representative sample of 1257 first year students conducted at the University of the North showed that 33 per cent of 85 per cent of the first year students experienced various adjustment problems.

Henning, Ey and Shaw (1998) studied the psychological distress; perfectionism and imposter feelings were assessed in 477 medical, dental, nursing and pharmacy students. Consistent with previous reports, the results showed that a higher than expected percentage of students (27.5%) were currently experiencing psychiatric levels of distress. Strong associations were found between current psychological distress, perfectionism and impostor feelings within each programme and these character traits were stronger predictors of psychological adjustment than most of the demographic variable associated previously with distress in health professional students.

Strange (1998) studied about family context variable and the development of self-regulation in college students. This paper proposes the conceptual framework based on attachment theory. A sample of 465 students was surveyed with 104-item students' attitudes and perception survey. Positive adjustment to the college is the one of the dimensions in this survey. Results show better adjustment for students living with their parents as well as for those living on their own.

The above studies indicate the student adjustment in various dimensions of personality like extroversion, neuroticism, parent attachment, college adjustment etc.

3. Hostel Environmental Adjustment

It includes the situational or environmental factors in a campus hostel. This category divided into the environmental factors and the related studies on hostels.

(i) Environmental Factors

The studies conducted on situational or environmental factors adopted for the literature.

Carlisle-Frank (1992) reviews literature on the psychological, sociological and environmental factors associated with relocation. It is argued that relocation is a complex personal, social and environmental transition that not only changes location of housing but also alters activities and domains. These changes associated with moving are enduring and affect almost every aspect of the individuals' life situation.

Terry (1994) conducted a longitudinal study of 243 students to examine the stable and situational influences on coping. After three sets of responses in a period of time, the results indicated that there was evidence that stable factors did influence coping behaviour.

The above studies showed that the situational factors influence the process of adjustment.

(ii) Related Studies on Hostels

The studies conducted on hostel students are mentioned in this portion.

Floyd (1988) examined the family experience and college residential adjustment. The sample consists of 42 undergraduates in living learning group. They found the possibility that early parental attention and orientation toward social inclusion would mediate the relationship between family socio-economic status and college living group satisfaction. Data did not support a mediation effect.

Takahashi and Majima (1994) investigated by using 26 weeks of longitudinal data on 61 Japanese female first year college students, this study examined how the pre established framework of social relationships of an individual student affect adjustment to the transition from home to the college campus dormitory. In the results, as predicted the age mate dominant type students more easily developed relationships with new age mates and reported fewer difficulties in making the transition than their family-dominant-type counterparts.

Barthelemy and Fine (1995) attempted to identify residence hall factors that enhance adjustment to college. The sample consists of 121 college students living in residence halls. In the results for both men and women personal support and group cohesiveness were positively correlated with most adjustment dimensions. Conflict was negatively related to social adjustment for both sexes, and to all adjustment dimensions for women. Also for women, group cohesiveness was positively related to academic adjustment and personal-emotional adjustment. For men, personal support and order were positively correlated with academic adjustment.

Bettencourt, Charlton, Eubanks and Kernahan (1999) investigated whether collective self-esteem development and residence hall membership predict adjustment to college in 142 first year students. Results show that academic adjustment at the end of first year in college was predicted by development in collective self-esteem. Development in collective self-esteem was associated with improvements in adjustment to college from first semester to the second semester. Results also show that residential group membership could have positive influences on adjustment. Implications of these findings are discussed in terms of their ramification for students academic adjustment, as well as for understanding the role of positively valued social identification with a context related group in enhancing overall positive adjustment in that context.

The above studies revealed that the social relationships, family, hostel factors influence the adjustment of students residing in hostel.

STUDIES IN INDIA

This section includes with the Indian studies on adjustment. Comparing to the western context, the Indian studies are few in number. The studies were again sub-categorised in to demographic, personality adjustment and hostel adjustment dimensions.

1. Demographic Variables

The demographic variables of the Indian studies consist of sex, nationality, faculty, rural/urban areas and economic status. The student adjustment studies related to the demographic variables from India taken for the literature.

(i) Sex

Only study related to the adjustment was located and suitable for the present study.

Lakshmi (1998) studied the adjustment of androgynous (male and female) persons in different areas such as home, health, social and emotional. The sample consists of 100 individuals of which 50 were androgynous and 50 were hyper masculine males and hyper feminine females drawn from different sections of society. Results revealed that the adjustment of androgynous persons was significantly better in all four areas than that of hyper masculine and hyper feminine females.

Thus the study indicated that the normal male and female students were better in overall adjustment.

(ii) Nationality

One study adopted from the literature, conducted on foreign students studying in Indian University.

Odera and Hasan (1995) studied about the problems of adjustment to a foreign culture. Out of 150 listed situations, 22 social situations were reported to encounter by 90 per cent of 38 foreign students. The conclusions revealed that the problems that face foreign students are neither eliminated nor reduced. Counselling is necessary for foreign students; if the problem is acute then psychiatrist help is also needed for better adjustment.

Thus the counselling programmes of the Indian Universities should be improvised for the international students.

(iii) Faculty

One study adopted from the Indian literature conducted on faculty.

Rajan, Ashrafullah and Rajan (1988) studied about the adjustment problems of professional and non-professional students. The sample consists of 346 college students out of which 131 professional and 212 non-professional students. The important findings are the non-professional science students have a better level of adjustment than the professional students only in the emotional area but not in the social and educational areas. The professional students have a better level of adjustment than the non-professional arts students in the educational area but not in the emotional area. The non-professional arts students have better level of adjustment than the professional students in the social area. The non-professional science students have a better level of adjustment than the non-professional arts students in the emotional and educational areas but not in the social area.

The study indicates the various differences among the different faculties in student adjustment.

(iv) Rural/Urban areas

The adjustment studies on student population conducted on areas or permanent place of residential location were taken from Indian literature.

Kasinath (1990) studied the factors underlying adjustment in Navodaya Vidayalayas. The study conducted on 68 students of which 50 boys and 18 girls, but the data of 20 urban and 28 rural students taken into consideration. The findings of this study indicates that there is no significant difference in the total adjustment scores of urban and rural, boys and girls studying in Navodaya Vidyalayas in respect of their emotional, social and educational adjustment.

Sujatha, Gaonkar, Khadi and Katarki (1993) conducted a study on factors influencing adjustment among urban and rural adolescents was carried out in Dharward block of Karnataka State. The sample consists of 300 students taken randomly out of 152 students from urban and 148 students from rural areas. The study revealed significant differences in the adjustment of male and female adolescent students of rural area. Early and late adolescents from both the urban as well as rural area did not differ significantly in their adjustment. Significant association was found between academic achievement and adjustment level among rural respondents.

Alexander and Packiam (1998) designed to find out the adjustment problems of male and female school going adolescents from two neighbouring and culturally similar groups, 157 students from Vellore town and nearby villages involved in the study. Findings revealed no significant difference in the proportion of maladjustment among the urban students. Urban adolescents have more problems than the rural students. Mother's education influences urban adolescent's adjustment.

The studies conducted on rural/urban areas and the adjustment factors on student populations were various conclusions in the above studies. Majority of studies indicates that there is a significant association between adjustment and rural/urban areas.

(v) Economic Status

This variable is an important one in the field of Indian Education. Most of the adjustment studies are interlinked with the socio-economic status of the students. Four studies are adopted from the Indian.

Khan (1991) examined the relationship of adjustment to personality factors like anxiety, ego strength, approval-seeking motive and personal background factors like socio-economic status, father's occupation, structure of family etc., among college students. The sample consists of 500 students out of 250 males and 250 females. The findings are based on the high and low scores (poor and better adjusted group) of the male and female respondents separately. Various personality and familial background factors have been found to affect on individuals adjustment.

Mohan and Kaur (1991) studied the adjustment of university research scholars in relation to their values and socio-economic status. The sample consists of 200 students out of 90 male and 110 female students. The adjustment inventory consists of questions in four areas of adjustment-home, health, social and emotional. Values were measured in terms of theoretical, economic, aesthetic, social, political and religious. The socio-economic status scale consists of questions pertaining of education, occupation and income of father. In the findings, adjustment was found to have a positive correlation with economic values and a negative correlation with religious values. However, no significant correlation was found between adjustment and SES. Faculty differences were found to be significant for home adjustment, emotional adjustment, total adjustment, theoretical values, aesthetic values, political values and SES. Sex was found to a significant determiner of health adjustment, emotional adjustment, and total adjustment, theoretical, aesthetic, social, political and religious values and socio-economic status.

Miya and Krishna (1996) examine the impact of socio-economic deprivation on adjustment of urban male college freshman. The sample consists of 166 deprived and 106 non-deprived students. Findings reveal that the deprived group had more health related adjustment problems than the non-deprived group. Home, social and emotional dimensions of adjustment could not discriminate between the deprived and the non-deprived groups. Biserial correlation analyses reveal that socio-economic deprivation had a significant positive relationship with health and emotional dimensions of adjustment.

Mishra and Singh (1998) determine the personality adjustment of graduate students belonging to high and low socio-economic status. A sample of 400 subjects, 200 male and female graduates of high SES, and 200 male and female graduates of low SES, completed the personality adjustment inventory. Results reveal significant difference between high SES and low SES graduates, in the case of both males and females, in all the areas of personality adjustment such as health, home, social, emotional and economic.

The economic status showed the influence on personality adjustment of the students from the conclusions of the above studies.

2. Personality Dimensions

The Indian literature adopted, from the different personality adjustment dimensions appropriate for the present study in this subcategory.

(i) Academic Adjustment

The Indian studies conducted on student adjustment with relation to academic aspects were included in this portion.

Sharma, Verma and Kumar (1989) studied about the relationship of achievement motivation, adjustment and self-concept with academic performance of the students at +2 stage. The sample consists of 155 students from Delhi. The results of the study revealed that out of three, two variables namely achievement motivation and adjustment had positive and significant relationship with academic performance. However, the self-concept of students was not found to be a facilitative or detrimental factor of academic achievement.

Ray (1992) studied the personality characteristics and adjustment variables related to academic achievement. The study conducted on 165 female college girls belonging to the families of high and low socio-economic status. The results concluded that home and health areas of adjustment influence academic achievement of female college students. Moreover, dominance, practical mindednesses, self-sufficiency, control over emotion, intelligence, and the need for achievement are the important consideration for successful scholastic achievement. Hence, adjustment that involves maturity in human behaviour influences academic achievement.

Sood (1992) examined the academic achievement in relation to adjustment. The sample consists of 120 pre engineering students of Ambala. Higher Secondary / Pre-university final marks were taken as achievement. It is found that there is no significant relationship between achievement and adjustment.

Tiwari and Pooranchand (1994) conducted a study of adjustment among high and low achieving adolescents. 100 students out of 50 high achievers and 50 low achievers participated in this study. The findings concluded that high and low achieving adolescents significantly differ in home, social and emotional areas of adjustment. However, they do not differ significantly in health and school adjustment.

The above studies indicated the relationships of academic adjustment of student adjustment.

(ii) Social Adjustment

The studies related to social aspects in Indian settings were adopted in this portion.

Rao and Yadav (1992) studied the adjustment problems of 240 adolescent girls in relation to family size and birth order. The results revealed that as the family size increased, the degree of satisfactory adjustment decreased. The second born in general, in all the families was found that well adjusted. The increase of family size with an addition of lateral birth orders after the second born, had more negative effect on the first born, consequently the third and fourth born are better adjusted than the first born in the areas of home, health, social, emotional and in general adjustment.

P.R. Chaudhury and Basu (1998) examined the impact of parent-child relationship on the school achievement and adjustment of 105 adolescent boys. The results indicated that the pattern of mothering, significantly influenced school adjustment. Both mothering and fathering styles were associated with academic success, particularly, rejection and neglect from parents were found to be highly detrimental.

Bajpai (1999) investigated the effect of caste belongingness on adjustment of high school girls. The study conducted on 400 high school girl students of which comprised of 176 general caste, 61 Backward caste, 134 scheduled tribe and 29 scheduled caste of

Madhya Pradesh Results shows that in the level of adjustment inventory that caste belongingness influence adjustment in different areas.

The above social factors influence the student adjustment in Indian context.

(iii) Related Studies on Personality Adjustment

The supported studies on personality adjustment of student populations are included in this portion.

Verma and Swain (1991) conducted a study to as certain whether self-concept of adolescent students is a determining factor of their personality adjustment. The sample of the study comprised of 200 subjects out of 100 males and 100 females. The present study attempted to investigate the differences in personality adjustment of adolescent students possessing high, average and low levels of self-concept. The findings of the study revealed that variations in self-concept produce differences in personality adjustment of adolescent students.

Kasinath (1991) conducted a study of adjustment between migrated Hindi and non-Hindi speaking students studying in Jawahar Navodaya Vidyalayas. The sample consists of 235 students among 52 urban/183 rural and 201 boys/ 34 girls and 197 non-Hindi speaking/38 Hindi speaking students. Results indicated that there are some variations in Hindi speaking and non-Hindi speaking students in the areas of Social, Educational and Emotional adjustments.

Chaudhary and Sinha (1992) examined the effect of extraversion and neuroticism on adjustment in four different areas of adjustment namely home, health, social and emotional adjustment of college student. Sample consists of 100 male students from Semi Urban Colleges. Results of high and low extraverts showed better social adjustment than did low extraverts. High and low neurotic students differed substantially in all the four areas of adjustment.

Singh (1992) investigated the student activism in relation to adjustment. The study was done on 200 students of post-graduate classes among 100 activists and 100 non-activists. The results revealed that the two groups of student activists and non-activists differed significantly in the area of different adjustments. The results further indicated that activists were generally poor in home, health, emotional, educational and overall adjustment while better in social adjustment in comparison to non-activist students.

Ponraj and Packiam (1993) conducted a study on adjustment problems of 50 adolescent students. The results revealed that girls were well adjusted in home, school, society and health in comparison with boys. Religion makes an impact on the adjustment of the adolescence in home, school, society and health. Caste is also influencing the adjustment of the adolescents.

Swami (1993) conducted a study on adjustment of 264 male/ 277 female orphan students in comparison with 264 male/277 female normal students. The conclusions are normal students were better adjusted than orphan students. Normal male and normal female students were better adjusted than the corresponding orphan males and orphan females. Thus sex had no effect on the relationship of adjustment of orphan and normal students. The adjustment of orphan male students was higher than the orphan females. The adjustment of normal female and normal male students was similar.

Hussain and Kumari (1995) examined the relationship of H.J. Eysenck's (1963) personality dimensions of psychoticism, extraversion and neuroticism with ego strength and adjustment. 100 male college students participated in this study. Ego strength was negatively related to psychoticism and neuroticism and positively but non-significantly related to extraversion. Some areas of adjustment were related positively and others negatively with psychotism, extraversion and neuroticism. There was a non-significant correlation between neuroticism and adjustment. High neuroticism/psychoticism was related to better adjustment. High ego-strength was related to lower psychoticism, neuroticism and greater extraversion.

The above studies indicated that many personality adjustment variables leads to student adjustment in a better way.

3. Adjustment to Hostel Environment

Mukhopadhyay, De, Chattopadhyay and Biswas (1996) examined the impact of socially disadvantaged conditions on the psychological arousal system. A sample of 120 women, aged 18 to 22 years was equally divided in to four groups; Institutionalised orphans, deaf and dumb subjects living in a hostel for the deaf (DDH), normal subjects residing in hostels (NH) and normal subjects residing at home (NRH). Results showed that the normal hostelmates are a little bit high in emotionality.

In review of literature on the two major areas of personality and hostel environmental adjustment has indicated the need to conduct further study in this area, in spite of consistent relationships being observed. The line of action suggested that adjustment of hostel students in various dimensions like personality and environmental factors. The present study makes a humble attempt in this direction. The methodology adopted to conduct the study is presented in the next chapter.

3

METHODOLOGY OF RESEARCH

This chapter describes the methodology adopted in the present study. It involves comparison of hostel students categorised into various individual factors on their personality and hostel adjustment scores and examining the correlations of certain personality adjustment variables with hostel environmental variables. More specifically it includes the comparison of hostel students in the aspects of age, sex, nationality, faculty, permanent place of residence, previous and present hostel experiences and economic status. The details of these variables and their measurements are presented in the following pages.

OBJECTIVES OF THE STUDY

1. To examine the personality of hostel students and the impact of individual factors on their personality.
2. To examine the hostel environmental adjustment of students and the impact of individual factors on hostel environmental adjustment.

3. To examine the impact of interactions among individual variables of age, gender and place of residence on personality and hostel environmental adjustment variables.
4. To examine the relationships between personality and hostel environmental adjustment dimensions.

HYPOTHESES OF THE STUDY

1. Individual variables will have a significant influence on personality.
2. Individual variables will have a significant influence on hostel adjustment.
3. The interactions of individual variables will have a significant influence on personality and hostel environmental adjustment.
4. Personality variables are expected to have a significant relationship with hostel environmental variables.

RESEARCH TOOLS OF THE STUDY

Personality and Hostel adjustment inventories were used for the present study. Both the research tools are culture fair for Indian situations and they are standardised inventories.

Personality Adjustment Inventory

Sharma (1972) has initially developed a pool of 75 items to measure personality adjustment. The preliminary tryout was conducted to a sample of 350 subjects with equal number of male and female subjects. On the basis of item analysis i.e., point biserial correlation values of each item, 54 items have been found significant at .01 level and were retained and the remaining 21 items were discarded. The investigator used the upper and lower 27 per cent of cases for item analysis.

The revised form of personality adjustment with 54 items was again administered to a different sample of 100 subjects of the same population and again the values of point biserial correlations were calculated and found the satisfactory significant values.

The final inventory consists of 54 items. After having gone through the various adjustment inventories, and the available literature and consultations with psychologists, six dimensions were identified: (1) Self pity; (2) Loneliness; (3) Emotionality; (4) Health adjustment; (5) Academic adjustment; and (6) Social adjustment. The personality adjustment inventory and the 6 dimensions of personality adjustment are given in the appendix.

The reliability index and reliability coefficient of the personality adjustment inventory were 0.83 and 0.63 respectively for the sample of 150 subjects in the test-retest method with an interval of 25 days. The validity coefficient was 0.81, when correlated with the scores of Ashthana, H.S.'s adjustment inventory.

In the personality adjustment inventory, beside every item, yes/no responses are present. 'Yes' responses were considered to be the correct answers i.e., the individual shows the neurotic tendency and the 'No' responses show otherwise. One mark was given to the 'Yes' answer and zero to the 'No' answer. The sum of scores shows the degree of neurotic tendency of the individual.

Hostel Adjustment Inventory

Krishnan and Sundaram (1992) initially developed a pool of 80 items to measure hostel adjustment. The preliminary tryout was conducted to two samples of 370 subjects and 200 subjects of professional courses college students, constituted on the basis of stratified random sampling technique, with due representation given to sex (Male and Female), native place (City, Town and Village), Community (forward, backward, scheduled caste and scheduled tribe) and course type.

Another try out of the hostel adjustment inventory having 80 items was administered to a sample of 300 students. They were arranged in ascending order on the basis of total scores. High and low hostel adjustment groups were formed by covering the top most hundred and bottom most hundred i.e., 27 per cent of upper and lower cases. Item analysis was done by the employment of test of significance of difference between means of the high and low hostel adjustment groups. 40 items have been found significant at 0.5 level and were retained and the remaining 40 items were eliminated.

The revised form of hostel adjustment with 40 items was again administered to a different sample of 200 subjects of the same population and again the values of item analysis were calculated and found the satisfactory significant values.

After having gone through the rules and regulations of various hostels and the available literature and consultation with a few wardens and psychologists, ten dimensions were identified: (1) room; (2) toilet; (3) food and dining hall; (4) adjustment with hostelmates and servants; (5) Health and Recreation; (6) Guest; (7) Information; (8) Crisis; (9) Financial; and (10) Spiritual adjustment. The reliability index and the reliability coefficient of split half method was 0.82 and 0.67 respectively and for test retest method the values were 0.83 and 0.69 for the sample of 200 subjects with an interval of one month. The validity coefficient was 0.78 when correlated between inventory scores and average rating scores of the respondents. The hostel adjustment inventory (Part: 'C' of the questionnaire) and the 10 dimensions of hostel adjustment are given in the appendix.

There are 20 positive and 20 negative items in this inventory. The item numbers of 20 positive items are 3, 6, 10, 11, 12, 20, 22, 23, 24, 25, 26, 27, 29, 32, 33, 34, 35, 37, 38 and 39. The item numbers of 20 negative items are 1, 2, 4, 5, 7, 8, 9, 13, 14, 15, 16, 17, 18, 19, 21, 28, 30, 31, 36 and 40 according to the serial order of the questionnaire.

For the 20 positive items, a descending order score (5/4/3/2/1) was given to the responses viz., always/often/some time/rarely/never, respectively. For the 20 negative items an ascending order score (1/2/3/4/5) was given to the responses, viz., always/often/sometime/rarely/never, respectively.

Hence, the hostel adjustment score of an individual may range between 40 and 200. The responses of the hostel students to the questionnaires were assigned weightage in accordance with the variable being measured under the wording of specific items.

VARIABLES OF THE STUDY

Three types of variables have been examined in the present study, namely, the individual, personality and hostel adjustment variables. The individual variables are age, sex, nationality, faculty, permanent place of residence, previous hostel experience, present hostel experience and economic status.

The personality adjustment variables are self-pity, loneliness, emotionality, health adjustment, Academic adjustment and social adjustment and the hostel adjustment variables are room, toilet, food and dining hall, hostelmates and servants, health and recreation, guest, information, crisis, financial and spiritual adjustments.

The details regarding these variables are provided in the following pages:

Individual Variables

The individual variables included in the present study are age, sex, nationality, faculty, and permanent place of residence, previous and present hostel experiences and economic status of the hostel students.

(i) Age

The minimum age for arts, science and law to study in Indian campus is 20+years. Whereas for medicine and engineering it is 17+years. In order to control the age, the researcher, selected the 3rd and 4th year students of medicine and engineering. The minimum age group of all students from different faculties for the present study is 20+years. Most of the student population was in between the age group of 20-28 years. Based on this aspect, it was categorised in to two groups i.e., below 25 years and 25 years and above with a gap of four years each according to the majority of student population.

Takahashi and Majima (1994) investigated by using 26 weeks of longitudinal data on 61 Japanese female first year college students, this study examined how the established framework of social relationships of an individual student affect adjustment to the transition from home to the college campus dormitory. In the results, the age mate dominant type students more easily developed relationships with new age mates and reported fewer difficulties in making the transition than their family dominant type counterparts

The study indicates that the age mate dominant females are better in social adjustment. The age factors up to certain extent influence the personality adjustment of hostel students.

(ii) Gender

It was the common gender differentiation in so many researches, In order to study the problem in detail; it is very essential to differentiate sex. As a recent trend in education and to uplift the woman education Indian Government implemented the rule of reservation that 1/3rd of the total seats were reserved for woman. On that aspect the comparative ratio in sex was almost equal in university student population. On these aspects, the researcher chooses the male as well as female students almost equal.

Street and Kromrey (1994) examined the differences in adjustment issues for male and female adolescents. They have concluded that, female students were more likely than males to experience difficulties with self-esteem, depression and anxiety. Males were more likely to experience difficulties with substance use. The study conducted by Lapsley, Rice and Shadid (1989) also concluded that sex differences are present, with women showing more psychological dependency than men.

Lopez (1991) examined that female students who reported high levels of marital conflict in their current family environments evidenced lower personal college adjustment. Rice (1992) examined previously reported sex differences in separation-individuation and college adjustment. They found that gender specific patterns of individuation adjustment emerged in freshman and junior years.

In Indian studies Lakshmi (1998) found the differences between androgynous and hyper masculine males and hyper feminine females. Mohan and Kaur, (1991) differentiate the sex based on different adjustment factors.

The above-mentioned studies indicate the sex variable influence the personality adjustment.

(iii) Nationality

This variable is the differentiation between the nations. In the university campus 51 students from the African and Asian countries were studying the courses in different faculties. So far no one studied the adjustment of foreign students in Andhra University. The researcher was interested to know the adjustment of foreign students in comparison with Indian students.

In India, Odera and Hasan (1995) studied about the problems of adjustment to a foreign culture. The conclusions revealed that the problems that are faced by foreign students are neither eliminated nor reduced. It seems that, there is hardly provision for counselling of foreign students and if counselling sources are available there is hardly any co-ordination between the counsellor and the authority in most of the Indian universities. The students who display deep emotional disturbances or the pathological systems require counselling at a deeper level and should be referred to a counselling psychologist or a clinical psychologist or in some cases to a psychiatrist.

The foreign studies done on International students are: Tanaka, Takai et al. (1994) concluded that Asian students were less adjusted than those of western and Latin American cultures. Kaczmarek, et al. (1994) found that the international students experienced more difficult transition than US students. Barrat and Huba (1994) found that the interpersonal relationships of the international students in an American community were positively correlated.

Abe, et al (1998) observed that students from Asian countries had more difficulty adjusting to campus life than international students from non-Asian countries.

All the above-mentioned foreign studies indicate that students of Asian countries suffered more with adjustment problems in foreign cultures whereas such problems are low in case of other continental students. The International students in Indian universities seek psychological counselling in transition. Consequently, the present study has taken up this issue for examination.

(iv) Faculty

The student population belonging to the university campus is categorised in to Arts, Science, Engineering, Medicine and Law faculties. In order to study the problem as a whole in the campus, it was suggested to choose more or less equal number of students for the present study among these five major faculties. By this detailed study, it can be understand the adjustments of each group and the comparisons among the five groups.

Mohan and Kaur (1991) studied the adjustment of Research scholars in the faculty-wise comparison. The faculty differences were found to be significant for home adjustment, emotional adjustment, and total adjustment. Similar study done by S.S. Rajan, Ashrafullah and V.N. Rajan (1988) concluded that non-professional science students have a better level of adjustment than the professional students only in the emotional area but not in social and emotional areas. The professional students have a better level of adjustment than the non-professional arts students in the educational area but not in the emotional area. The non-professional arts students have better level of adjustment than the professional students in the social area. The non-Professional science students have a better level of adjustment than the non-professional arts students in the emotional and educational areas but not in the social area. The above Indian studies indicated the variations in the different levels of adjustments. Hence this faculty variable is important for the present study.

(v) Permanent Place of Residence

Most of the students came from the rural areas to study higher education in university campus. The local area for the campus belongs to seven districts of Srikakulam, Vijayanagaram, Visakhapatnam East Godavari, West Godavari, Krishna, Guntur and Prakasam. The majority of coastal area includes number of villagės, Mandals, towns and cities. Villages and Mandals constitute rural area and towns and cities constitute urban area. The place of residence i.e. rural or urban was an important variable to study in detail and comparison between them.

Kasinath's (1990) study indicates that there is no significant difference in the total adjustment scores of urban and rural, boys and girls studying in Navodaya Vidyalayas in respect of their emotional, social and educational adjustment. Sujatha Gaonkar et al, (1993) study revealed significant differences in the adjustment of male and female adolescent students of rural area. Early and late adolescents from both the urban as well as rural area did not differ significantly in their adjustment. Significant association found between academic achievement and adjustment level among rural respondents. Alexander and Packiam, (1998) study revealed no significant difference in the proportion of maladjustment among the urban students. Urban adolescents have more problems than the rural students. The above Indian studies indicate that there is an influence of area on adjustment. This variable is also included in the present study.

(vi) Previous Hostel Experience

This variable includes the experience in hostel either in school, under graduation or graduation and no experience in these three levels. Many private residential schools and junior colleges established in the areas of university zone. Some government hostels established for minority students. The study belongs to the students of hostels and it was essential to know about the previous hostel experience. The measurement includes the adjustment of experienced and inexperienced students and the comparisons between them.

The researcher wants to know whether any improvement for the previous hostel experience students than inexperience hostel students and also to know the differences in the significant dimensions of adjustment. Some students got experience only in school, some students got experience in only in under graduation and some students got experience only in graduation. There was a possibility of experience in school and under graduation and graduation and the total experience in these three levels. Students who have earlier experience have more chances of better adjustment than those with no experience in hostel life. To know the reasons for this dimension, to consider these above said hypotheses for the present, study it was necessary to test this individual variable. On that rationale the researcher chooses and selected this previous hostel experience variable.

The researcher not located the previous studies from Indian literature concerned to this type of measurement of variable; it could be useful for the other hostel studies also.

(vii) Present Hostel Experience

The present hostel experience considered was the duration of the respective course in the university campus. The duration of arts and science post graduation studies is two years, for law it is three years and for medical and engineering students it is four years. Sometimes in some students continue their practical examination like house surgeons in case of medical students, apprenticeship in engineering students, a possibility of staying one more year in hostels. On the whole, a period of stay in hostels for the campus students had one to five years.

The researcher wants to test whether any improvement in hostel adjustment from year to year or whether any fluctuations among the duration of years and also to know the differences in the significant value of adjustment dimensions year by year. To test those above-mentioned hypotheses, it was rationale for selecting the present hostel experience variable.

The researcher has not traced the above-mentioned variable from the Indian literature; the measurement of this variable would be useful for further hostel studies.

(viii) Economic Status

It is an important variable in Indian situations. This individual variable of the hostel students can be also noted as annual income of the family. This variable is divided in to five groups i.e., below Rs. 10, 000/-, between Rs. 10, 000/- to Rs. 25, 000/-, between Rs. 25, 000/- to Rs. 50, 000/- between to Rs. 1,00,000/- and above Rs. 1,00,000/-. The first group of students is poor students, the second, third and fourth group of students belongs to middle class I, II and III categories and the fifth group of students are from rich status.

Some Indian studies were done on the adjustment of students based on economic status and some studies were clubbed with social status along with economic status were done on the adjustment of students related to socio-economic status. Khan (1991) found that socio-economic status of the family has been significantly associated with adjustment of high and low female groups. Mohan and Kaur (1991) found the socio-economic status and adjustment of university of Research Scholars was related insignificantly. Miya and Krishna (1996) revealed that the socio-economic deprivation had a significant positive relationship with health and emotional dimensions of adjustment. Mishra and Singh (1998) found that personality adjustment was influenced by the socio-economic status of graduate students. Results reveal significant differences between high SES and low SES graduates, in the case of both males and females, in all the areas of personality adjustment such as health, home, social and emotional adjustments.

The above studies indicate that there is a relationship between socio-economic status and adjustment of students. Hence this variable adopted for the present study to observe the relationship between adjustment and economic status of the hostel students.

Personality Variables

The personality variables included in the present study are self-pity, loneliness, emotionality, health adjustment, academic adjustment and social adjustment.

(i) Self-pity

This variable measures the degree of maladjustment related to self-pity. The person himself suffers a lot by thinking inferiorly. The items related to disappointments, pitiable conditions. A feeling of sadness, inferiority complex and downward feeling measures the self-pity of the students. In self-pity condition, the student suffers a lot and it will become an obstacle for the student to achieve the desirable goal.

Rim (1989) found that sex was found to be a moderating variable, with males and females, results often differing in self-confrontation. Aspinwall and Taylor (1992) indicated that a two-year followup study of self-esteem and control predicted greater motivation and higher grades. Ichiyama, et al. (1993) found that the self-concealment was significantly correlated with self reported anxiety, depression, shyness and negative self-esteem. The tendency to self-conceal was also found to be differently related to the adjustment variable as a function of sex. Graziano, Jensen- Campbell and Finch (1997) examined and found that the self can be conceptualised as a mediating agent that translates personality into situated goal-directed activities and adaptation. Greenier, Kernis et al, (1999) concluded that negative and positive events had a greater impact on the self-feelings of individuals with unstable as opposed to stable self-esteem.

All the above-mentioned studies indicated that the self-feelings of the individuals influence the person's adjustments in every aspect. It is an important thing to measure the self-feelings of the student community in the hostel atmosphere in the present study.

(ii) Loneliness

This variable measures the degree of maladjustment caused by loneliness. The items related to the negative aspect i.e., the felling of lonely, haunted by aloneness, fear of alone and stay alone measures the maladaptive behaviour caused by the loneliness of the person. Such type of negative feelings of the individual creates maladjustment in the hostel at the sametime it was a big hindrance for the student.

Clinton and Anderson (1999) studied the social and emotional loneliness, gender differences and relationships with self-monitoring and perceived control. This study provides insight into these overlooked dimensions of loneliness. For men, emotional loneliness caused by lack of intimacy with friends. For women, emotional loneliness was inversely related to perceived control. Sensitivity to the expressive behaviour of others was significantly and inversely correlated with emotional loneliness only when individuals had high scores on the perceived control scale.

The above study indicated that due to lack of certain social relationships, the loneliness caused maladjustment to the person. For a student living in a group in a hostel, it is very important to measure the maladjustment behaviour caused by loneliness. Man is a social animal, he cannot live alone. He has to develop some positive relationships with fellow hostelmates in certain aspects i.e., communication about the academic matters, placements, information regarding hostels or campus etc. The ignorance behaviour of others is not a sign of good adjustment in a hostel. This variable is very important for the present study.

(iii) Emotionality

This variable is an important one and plays a leading role in one's adjustment to his environment. An individual is said to be emotionally adjusted if he is able to express his emotions in a proper way at a proper time. It requires ones balanced emotional development and proper training in expressing emotions. In extreme cases, a student must seek balance between the extremes of repression on the one hand and uncontrolled emotional expressiveness on the other; otherwise he becomes the victim rather than the master of this most potent force in his personality.

The items of this variable include the excitement, fear, cry, nervousness, anxiety and temperament. High scores on emotionality are found both among students who are overtly nervous and excitable and those who present an unexpressive front to the world. Counselling alone however cannot do the entire job. The student must also find more effective action patterns than he has in the past through which to express his feelings. So the hostel students of high emotionality are recommended for the counselling cell in psychology department of university campus.

Gerdes and Mallinckrodt (1994) studied emotional, social and academic adjustment of college students. It's a longitudinal study of retention in the six years of duration. Results indicate that two different sets of items best discriminated among good standing students among poor standing students. Generally emotional and social adjustment items predicted attrition as well or better than academic adjustment items.

In Indian studies Mohan and Kaur (1991) found the faculty differences in emotional adjustment and sex was found to a significant determinant of emotional adjustment. Tiwari and Pooranchand (1994) concluded the significant difference in high and low achieving students in emotional adjustment. S.S. Rajan, Ashrafullah and V.N. Rajan (1988) studied the adjustment problems of professional and non-professional college students and found the differences in emotional adjustment Mukhopadhya et al. (1996) concluded that the normal hostelmates are a little bit high in emotionality.

All the above-mentioned studies indicate that the emotionality variable influence much in student adjustment. It is a reasonable and rational variable to measure in the present study.

(iv) Health Adjustment

This dimension measures the degree of maladjustment in health. A high score on health adjustment means that the student has reported that he has not had a history of physical illness and that the physical ailments he may have had, have not bothered him sufficiently to cause discomfort or that he has developed an accepting attitude toward them.

It should be emphasised that the health adjustment scores are dependent upon the accuracy of the students' knowledge of his own health history and on the amount of discomfort that his ailments may have caused him.

The items related to the weakness, restlessness, sleeplessness, headaches, and feelings of physical suffering and anxiety about health. The maladjustment creates in the hostel if the student suffers more with the problems. At that time, it was advised to consult the dispensary physicians of south and north campuses.

Leong et al, (1990) found that Asian students in foreign culture showed greater difficulties with memory and hallucinations. Iwata (1994) found that higher intolerance for waiting stress was linked with greater physical and psychological symptoms and with maladjusted personality. Bernard et al, (1996) found the significant relationship between health and personality factors.

In Indian studies Mohan and Kaur (1991) in their investigation, sex was found to a significant determiner of health adjustment. Ray (1992) found that health adjustment influence academic achievement of female college students. Odera and Hasan (1995) studied about the problems of foreign students in Indian University. They suggested that the students who display deep emotional disturbances or the pathological systems require counselling at a deeper level and should be referred to counseling psychologist or a clinical psychologist or in some cases to a psychiatrist.

All the above-mentioned studies indicate that the health adjustment dimension influence the personality adjustment. There is a popular saying that the 'Sound mind in a sound body' so that the good health adjustment leads to good personality adjustment. This variable reasonably selected to measure the health of the hostel students for the present study.

(v) Academic Adjustment

This dimension measures the degree of maladjustment in academic aspects. Those students' wants to seek the high achievements in educational aspects needs better academic adjustment. The items related to the problem of attention, self torture for finding a solution, shyness of getting less marks, delay in coming to decision, lack of self confidence and trouble in answering etc. If the student suffers more of any of these aspects it creates maladjustment in academic aspect.

Smith and Baker (1987) concluded a relationship between academic and college adjustments and the adjustment problems associated with lack of academic major. Chartrand (1990) found that self-evaluation and commitment to the student role both had a direct effect on student role congruence, which in turn had a direct effect on academic performance and personal distress. Brooks and DuBois (1995) showed that although individual variables were related most strongly to adjustment, environmental variables made significant incremental contributions to prediction of academic and psychological adjustment.

In Indian studies K. Sharma, Verma and Kumar (1989) revealed that an achievement motivation and adjustment had positive and significant relationship with academic performance. Ray (1992) concluded that adjustment which involves maturity in human behaviour influence academic achievement. Sood (1992) found that there is no significant relationship between achievement and adjustment. Tiwari and Pooranchand (1994) concluded that high and low achieving adolescents significantly differ in home, social and emotional areas of adjustment.

The majority of above studies mentioned that the academic adjustment influence the personality adjustment of the students. Thus the academic adjustment variable measures the hostel students academic adjustment, has taken for the present study.

(vi) Social Adjustment

Social adjustment requires the development of social qualities and virtues in an individual. It also requires that one should be social enough to live in harmony with his social beings and feel responsibility and obligations towards his fellow beings, in hostel as well as in campus.

The items related the disturbances from people, hostility on people, hurt by others, difficulty in talking, irritation on members and nervous in meeting with opposite sex etc. The social adjustment dimension measures the degree of maladjustment in social situations. It is an important dimension in hostel situations.

Schweitzer et al (1991) used the utilisation focussed evaluation model, to evaluate the outcomes of an orientation seminar on early adjustment of college entering freshmen. Findings support the use of a freshman seminar as an intervention for promoting early academic and social adjustment to college life. The seminar seemed successful at increasing student's knowledge of the university, providing available support services and promoting adjustment to the campus social environment. Same authors in 1993 declared that students with low goal instability who perceived a high level of support had higher levels of semester-end adjustment than students who perceived a low level of support. The former used the available social support, both within and out side the classroom, to more effectively adjust to the university environment. Students with moderate levels of goal instability were not affected by social support. Robbins et al (1993) also support the above study. Zakahi et al (1993) concluded that the moderate or high communication apprehension to more quickly adjust to a new social environment.

In Indian studies Singh (1992) concluded that the student activists were generally poor in home, health, and emotional, educational and overall adjustment while better in social adjustment. Tiwari and Pooranchand (1994) concluded that the high and low achieve significantly differ in social adjustment. Rajan, Arrafuallah and Rajan, (1988) concluded the professional and non-professional college students significantly differ in social adjustment. Mishra and Singh (1998) concluded that the low and high socio-economic students significantly differ in social adjustment.

The above studies showed the variable social adjustment influence on personality adjustment of hostel students. This variable measures the social relationships in hostel adopted for the present study.

Dimensions of Hostel Adjustment

In personality adjustment dimensions, the measurement were done by the degree of maladjustment, where as in hostel adjustment dimensions, the degree of adjustment should be measured. There are ten dimensions in hostel adjustment related to hostel environment. They are Room, Toilet, Food and dining hall, Hostelmates and servants, Health and recreation, Guest, Information, Crisis, Financial and Spiritual adjustments.

(i) Room

Room is a place of residence in a hostel. It constitutes with other roommates, material and furniture. The room adjustment is an adjustment to the above said aspects. The measurement of room adjustment items related to roommates, electrical appliances of the room, furniture, material and study hours etc. The high scores in this dimension indicate the better room adjustment. It is the first aspect of environment and every student spends half of the day in room. This primary aspect of adjustment with room leads to adjust with other factors.

The student has to adjust with fellow roommates and maintain good social relationships with them. Secondly the student has to utilise the furniture like tables, chairs and material in a proper condition. The negligence or mishandling leads to loss of apparatus and those cause inconvenience to the other roommates. In using the electrical appliances also, like fans or lights, gentle maintenance is needed. Using high voltage electrical appliances like electric stoves, electric water heaters, electric iron boxes etc., cause heavy load for burning of the fuses. Such type of mishandling leads to inconvenience to other fellow students.

Hence this dimension reasonably selected for the measurement of room adjustment in hostel students.

(ii) Toilet

The toilet adjustment measures the fresh up of the students. The measuring items related to toilets, bathrooms, water, taps, works of scavengers, skid, flush etc. Generally in hostels common bathrooms meant for every student. It one student properly utilise the things in this aspect, the other student feel comfortable. This adjustment is a collective adjustment in the hostel. Flush of water after using the toilet, utilise the taps in a proper condition, using appropriate quantity of water without wasting, careful in case of slipping or skid in bathroom, sometimes monitor the works of scavengers are the proper adjustments of the students.

If a student adjusted better in toilet, he will adjust better in health, cleanliness etc. In higher education hostels, especially in university campus, students use properly and at the same time the sub staff or supervisors check the works in a clean manner. In some training institutes of mentally retarded, they stress on the aspects of toilet training for the retarded children. The researcher not traced literature based on this dimension from both foreign and Indian studies. However, the dimension is one of the key factors in hostel, quite suitable in choosing and selecting for the measurement for the present study.

(iii) Food and Dining Hall

Students attend for breakfast for morning times, lunch in afternoons and dinner in evenings. The dishes include the south Indian foods like rice, dal, rasam, chatni and sambar. For non-vegetarian students eggs and chicken curry will be served. Chief Wardens inspect the food material and maintain the quality of food.

For measurement of this dimension, the properly adjusted student takes food to his satisfaction or otherwise due to noises of the atmosphere may be not satisfied. For Indian student this type of food is common. Whereas for foreign students, certain adjustment would be necessary. Furukawa (1997) conducted a study on Japanese students studying in abroad. One of the conclusion in this study was food had the greatest impact on the intercultural adjustment.

The above study indicates that Indian food had the impact on foreign student's adjustment. To know the measurement of this variable, taken for the present study.

(iv) Hostelmates and Servants

This variable measures the social relationships in the hostel. The items related to mess boys, cooks, and watchmen, room boys, warn the servants, tip the servants, ragging, friendship with servants etc. Better adjustment leads to high score in this dimension. It was advised to maintain harmonious relationship with hostelmates and at the same time make the servants to work for the welfare of the hostel. It was not good to rag the new entrants and make friendships with servants. Those things spoil the dignity of student.

Takahashi and Majima (1994) studied about the social relationships in the college campus dormitory. They concluded that age mate dominant type students more easily developed relationships with new age mates. Barthelemy and Fine (1995) attempted to identify residence hall factors that enhance adjustment to college. The results concluded that for both men and women personal support and group cohesiveness were positively correlated with most adjustment dimensions. Conflict was negatively related to social adjustment for both sexes, and to all adjustment dimensions for women.

In Indian studies Singh (1992) Tiwari and Pooranchand (1994) Rajan, Asrafullah and Rajan (1988) also supported the social relationships with other hostilities influence personality adjustment. On the basis of the above studies this variable selected for the present study.

(v) Health and Recreation

In previous personality adjustment dimensions, health adjustment dimension measures the self-health adjustment.

Whereas this health and recreation dimension measures the health adjustment related to hostel environments. The items related to cosmetics, cleanliness, drinking water, dress and exercise students who are good in this aspect maintain good health habits. Maintaining the room cleanly use boiling water during illness, avoiding others dress or cosmetics and exercise with the available furniture in the hostel are the good health and recreation habits of well-adjusted students.

Apart from these, sports, music, yoga, gym all these habits gives pleasure for the mind of the student in elimination of stress especially for science and technology students. Those students who utilise those things properly have got good adjustment in this dimension.

In Indian studies Mohan and Kaur (1991) in their investigation, sex was found to a significant determiner of health adjustment. Ray (1992) found that health adjustment influence academic achievement of female college students.

The above-mentioned studies indicate that health and recreation dimension influence adjustment. There is a popular saying 'health is wealth". The variable health and recreation reasonably selected to measure in hostel students for the present study.

(vi) Guest

This dimension measures the adjustment towards guests. There is no provision to entertain guests in to the hostels, but the close associates like parents, relatives or outside friends have a chance to consult the students in hostel. The measuring items related to entertain plenty of guests, accommodate permitted guests and engage guests during stipulated hours constitute the guest adjustment. Entertain plenty of guest is not a good adjustment, to accommodate the permitted guests and engage guests during stipulated hours are better adjustments to certain extent.

The implementation of this dimension has done for the two aspects. The student has to adjust in handling the guests without disturbing his time schedules related to academic affairs and the permitted guest not causes a discomfort to the other fellow students.

It was the responsibility of the student to look over his guests that not to create any nuisance to the other hostel students.

The researcher not located the studies done on this dimension. This dimension indicates the more information related to environment in hostel for the present study.

(vii) Information

This dimension measures the adjustment towards information. The measuring items related to leave application for availing leave, inform the authorities for a stay outside and checking the notice board are included in information dimension. The student has to know the information about the hostel and intimate his information to the authorities of hostel in case of leave or for a stay outside the campus are the better adjustments.

Most of the students came from very far places, to study in university campus. It is the responsibility of the authorities to look over their welfare and at the same time they will act in a mediating authorities in between student and their parents. In such type of situations occurred, the student has to adjust for information dimension and give his information to the authorities.

The researcher not located the literature related to this dimension, but it is suitable for measuring the environmental situations in hostel, for the present study.

(viii) Crisis

This dimension measures the crisis. The measuring items related to the scarcity of water and room crisis when the authorities demand to vacate. Utilising the minimum water during scarcity and handover the rooms when the authorities demand are the better adjustments in crisis. Generally the authorities demand to vacate the room only after completion of the courses.

Sometimes in summer season, in the climatic conditions of drought, every hostel suffers with the scarcity of water. The municipal tankers supply water to the hostels. At such type of conditions, utilising minimum water for needs is the better adjustment in crisis. In case of room also, handover to the authorities in completion of courses is the better adjustment. The researcher not located the related literature on this dimension but this dimension suitable for Indian setting, selected for the present study.

(xi) Financial Adjustment

This dimension measures the financial adjustment of hostel students. This is one of the important dimensions for Indian student. The measuring items related to saving money, loans, paying fines, spending money etc., included in this dimension. Availing loans from others, paying fines to the hostel, spending too much for entertainments are the maladjusted aspects for the student. Whatever it may be proper usage of money and keep some amount in reserve are some what good habits of financial adjustment.

In the list of individual variables, the economic status of the hostel students' measures the adjustments related to rich, middle class and poor status students. Whereas this variable related to hostel adjustment is the maintenance of financial aspects in the hostel. The proper handling of financial matter leads to better adjustment in the hostel. The misuse of money leads to maladjustment of the students.

Thus, this variable selected for the present study to measure the financial adjustments of hostel students.

(x) Spiritual Adjustment

This dimension measures the spiritual adjustment of hostel students. The hostel students got different ritual practices according to their culture or by socialisation. The better spiritual adjustment has not to criticise others ritual practices in hostel.

Tobacyk and Driggers (1989) investigated the self-monitoring as a moderator of relationships between traditional religious belief and personality adjustment. The results suggest that low self-monitors show the strongest adaptive effects of religious belief on personality adjustment.

In Indian study Ponraj and Packiam (1993) conducted a study on adjustment problems of adolescent boys. The results revealed that girls were well adjusted in comparison with boys. Religion makes an impact on the adjustment of the adolescence in home, school, society and health aspects.

The above studies indicate that the spiritual adjustment influence the personality adjustment of the students. This dimension selected for the measurement of spiritual adjustment in hostel students for the present study.

SAMPLE OF THE STUDY

The researcher used the "Stratified random sampling" technique for sample collection. The total questionnaires were distributed were 1000 out of which 556 filled questionnaires were considered as sample by eliminating the unfilled and partially filled questionnaires. The final sample (N=556) selected for the present study. Among the sample, the strength of arts students was 129 with 76 male and 53 female students. The strength of science students was 122 out of 71 male and 51 female students. The strength of engineering students was 105 with 51 male and 54 female students. The strength of medical students was 100 with 51male and 49 female students. The strength of law students was 100 with an equal distribution of 50 each for male and female groups.

The total sample includes the totality of 40 foreign students were from different nations studying different courses. Out of 40 students 38 were male and 2 were female students.

In overall view 2,688 were male students and 1,046 were female students with the totality of 3,734 students were residing in hostels. A group of 1,940 students were selected for the present study. The sample includes 299 male and 257 female students (N=556), which constitute a 28 per cent sample from selected group.

DATA COLLECTION

Data collected from the hostels of Andhra University, Visakhapatnam. Engineering male and female hostels, Lawmen's hostels are located at the north campus of the university whereas arts and science male hostels located at the south campus. Entire ladies hostels located at beach side for arts, science, law and some engineering students.

The data from medical students collected from the Andhra Medical College Men's Hostel and Andhra Medial College Women's Hostel, King George Hospital, Visakhapatnam.

The List of Hostels

Nagarjuna, Satavahana, Sadharma Sadana and Siddartha hostels in the south campus located for the arts subject's male students with the total strength of 769 including the strength of diploma holders.

Sri Krishnadevaraya, Harshavardhana, Vivekavinyasa, Vinaya Vihara and Ashoka Vardhana hostels belongs to the science subject male students with the strength of 758 including the strength of part time diploma holders.

Block 1, Block 2, Block 3, Block 4, Block 5, Block 6, Block 7 and P.G. Block hostels located for the students of engineering and technology in north campus. Among the blocks, block V belongs to the female students' hostel whereas the remaining hostels meant for the male students. The total strength of all these hostels was 1,013 with full time students.

The Ladies hostels located at beach side, beside the Bay of Bengal. There are four ladies hostels viz., Old Block, New Block, Modern Block and Latest Block with the total strength of 687 including arts, science, engineering and law students.

Andhra medical college men's hostel located at the outside the campus and Andhra medical college women's hostel located at King George Hospital with the total strength of 371 medical students.

Samatha and Mamatha Hostels meant for the law male students established in north campus whereas the P.G. Block located in south camp for M.L. students. The total strength of all the three hostels was 136 students.

The data collected form the hostels in the months of November and December 1999. The total strength of the hostels at that time was noted.

Selected Group from Population

The total strength of hostel students was approximately 3,734. The students of part time diploma courses, the part-time students and students of below one-year courses were eliminated, due to their stay in the hostels was temporary during the vacation.

In case of medical and engineering students the age below 20 years students were eliminated because the other course i.e., for arts, science and law the minimum age is 20+ years. This was done for the maintenance of the homogeneity of the students' age in the present study.

The final group after selection was approximately 1,940 students from pure arts, science, medical, engineering and law students.

Administration of the Questionnaires

The researcher administered the questionnaires individually and sometimes by group according to the convenience. The subjects were asked to complete the columns of age, sex, and nationality etc., related to individual information printed on the second page of the questionnaire. The researcher read the instructions loudly appearing on the beginning of each inventory in part A, part B and part C-sections. After the subjects read out the instructions silently, the difficulties were asked and removed. Then the subjects were asked to begin marking the items. There is no time limit for marking the three parts, but normally 30-45 minutes were required to complete the total questionnaire. In some instances, the researcher explains the questions in the inventory in regional language Telugu in certain cases of subjects belongs to the background of 'Telugu' as medium of instruction.

Language of the Questionnaire

The study held in Visakhapatnam of South India, and the mother tongue of this region is 'Telugu' language. According to the educational systems of India, the national language 'Hindi' and international language 'English' should be taught from secondary level along with regional language.

The students of higher education and professional education in university campus have had and experience of five to ten years in English vocabulary. The students feel no difficulty in reading as well as understanding the questionnaire in English language as it self. The researcher clarified the doubts of the Telugu medium background students whenever they ask for the meaning. Very few students asked for the translation but the majority of students answered in English. The language used in the questionnaire was very simple, and every Indian student can understand it.

Kasinath (1991) conducted a study of adjustment between migrated Hindi and Non-Hindi speaking students. The results drawn NHS students are better emotionally, socially and educationally adjusted than HS students.

This study indicates that the language has its own significance in the adjustment of the students.

ANALYSIS OF DATA

The main objective of the present study was to examine the personality adjustment of hostel students. To achieve this objective the sample of 556 hostel students has to be categorised in to various factors like age, sex, nationality, faculty, permanent place of residence, previous and present hostel experiences and economic status of the hostel students.

The data collected from hostel students was analysed as follows:

1. t-tests were conducted to examine the significance of differences in mean scores of personality and hostel adjustments across the individual variables like age, sex, nationality, permanent place of residence and previous hostel experience;
2. One-way analyses of variances (ANOVA) tests were conducted to examine the significance of differences in mean scores of personality and hostel adjustments across faculties, present hostel experience in years and economic status of the students;
3. Multivariate analyses of variances (MANOVA) tests were conducted to examine the significance of differences of interaction of age and gender, interaction of age and place of residence and interaction of gender and place of residence on personality and hostel environmental adjustments;

4. Pearson's product moment cocfficient of correlation's were conducted between the personality adjustment variables and hostel adjustment variables and inter correlations for the both independent variables. These analyses would provide information regarding the relationships between the variables.

The next chapter followed the complete information with regard to results.

4

RESULTS AND DISCUSSION

The discussion of the results of the present study is presented in this chapter. The results are discussed according to the outcomes of the tables. The results are discussed in four sections of the following pages. The results and discussion of the study are presented in this chapter. The data has been analysed to examine:

- The personality factors of hostel students and the impact of individual factors on their personality;
- The hostel environmental adjustment of students and the impact of individual factors on hostel environmental adjustment;
- The interactions of individual variables on personality and hostel environmental adjustment variables;
- The relationship between personality and hostel environmental adjustment variables.

The results taken together would explain the relationships between personality and hostel environmental adjustment with the support variables on hostel students. The results and discussion are presented in four sections of the following pages:

- *Section I* includes the results and discussion relating to the influence of individual variables on personality dimensions;
- *Section II* includes the results and discussion regarding the influence of individual variables on hostel environmental adjustment variables;
- *Section III* includes the results and discussion regarding the interactions of individual variables on personality and hostel environmental adjustment variables;
- *Section IV* includes findings and discussion regarding the relationships between different independent variables.

SECTION – I

PERSONALITY DIMENSIONS

The personality scores indicate the degree of maladjustment in hostel students. Higher mean scores indicate the degree of maladjustment in the respective dimensions.

1. Comparison Across Age

The preliminary analysis of the data involved the comparison of the personality variables across the age groups i.e., Age below 25 years and Age 25 years and above. The mean scores and t-value are tabulated in Table 4.1. (*See on next page*)

The result points out that the emotionality variable significantly influences the two age groups. Students of 25 years of age and above group are significantly less emotional than Age group of below 25 years. It shows that the high age group adjusted better with regard to emotionality.

It is possible that younger students, due to lack of proper knowledge in experience the environmental situations of the hostel the age groups of below 25 years students were low comparatively with the 25 years and above group. Mukhopadhyay, *et.al.* (1996) in their study explained that the normal hostel students' emotionality would be increased in their transition. Takahashi and Majima (1994) found that the age mate dominant students developed relationship easily. It was a better social adjustment of the age mate dominant students are adjusted better due to their age dominance and the early transition cause emotional increase in the age group of below 25 years students.

Table 4.1

Age and Personality

(N= 556)

Dimensions	*Mean & S.D.*	*Age below 25 yr. (N=414)*	*Age 25 and above (N=142)*	*t values*
1. Self Pity	Mean	6.07	5.68	1.39
	S.D.	2.91	2.72	
2. Loneliness	Mean	1.47	1.46	0.12
	S.D.	1.10	1.14	
3. Emotionality	Mean	4.25	3.81	2.02*
	S.D.	2.16	2.36	
4. Health Adjustment	Mean	2.84	3.04	1.19
	S.D.	1.76	1.63	
5. Academic Adjustment	Mean	3.23	3.38	0.91
	S.D.	1.54	1.69	
6. Social Adjustment	Mean	3.81	3.84	0.12
	S.D.	2.06	2.37	

* $P< 0.05$

** $P< 0.01$

The other dimensions like self-pity, loneliness, health adjustment, academic adjustment and social adjustment are statistically not significant.

2. Comparison Across Sex

The mean scores of personality dimensions across the male and female students are presented in Table 4.2. The comparison of the scores indicates that the two sex groups of hostel students differ statistically on loneliness, emotionality and academic adjustment dimension.

Table 4.2

Gender and Personality

(N= 556)

Dimensions	*Mean & S.D.*	*Males (N=299)*	*Females (N=257)*	*t Values*
1. Self Pity	Mean	5.77	6.20	1.71
	S.D.	2.86	2.86	
2. Loneliness	Mean	1.35	1.61	2.83**
	S.D.	1.04	1.17	
3. Emotionality	Mean	3.86	4.46	3.22**
	S.D.	2.30	2.08	
4. Health Adjustment	Mean	2.98	2.80	1.23
	S.D.	1.67	1.80	
5. Academic Adjustment	Mean	3.41	3.11	2.19*
	S.D.	1.68	1.44	
6. Social Adjustment	Mean	3.81	3.84	0.15
	S.D.	2.16	2.12	

* $P < 0.05$.

** $P < 0.01$.

The mean scores on loneliness, academic adjustment and emotional adjustment are different across the male and female students. This observation indicates that female students feel lonely and emotionally low adjusted but academic adjustment was better than males. Generally female students suffer more emotionally in hostels due to lack of self-adjustment at the same time they feel lonely when away from homes. Lapsley, et al., (1989) and Street and Kromrey (1994) studies support the results in this aspect.

Whereas in academic adjustment, female students were strong. They spend much time on education, study and attending to classes in university whereas these activities are comparatively low in male students.

3. Comparison Across Nationality

The scores of the personality adjustment dimensions in comparison across the nationality i.e., foreign students and Indian students are computed and tabulated in Table 4.3.

Table 4.3

Nationality and Personality

(N= 556)

Dimensions	*Mean & S.D.*	*Foreign Students (N=40)*	*Indian Students (N=516)*	*t Values*
1. Self Pity	Mean	5.27	6.02	1.59
	S.D.	2.58	2.88	
2. Loneliness	Mean	1.45	1.47	0.14
	S.D.	1.10	1.11	
3. Emotionality	Mean	3.02	4.22	3.32**
	S.D.	1.79	2.23	
4. Health Adjustment	Mean	2.85	2.90	0.18
	S.D.	1.56	1.74	
5. Academic Adjustment	Mean	2.67	3.32	2.50*
	S.D.	1.65	1.56	
6. Social Adjustment	Mean	3.50	3.85	0.99
	S.D.	1.58	2.18	

* $P < 0.05$.

** $P < 0.01$.

The mean scores are recorded in the respective dimension. It can be observed that the statistically significant values obtained for the emotionality dimension ($t = 3.32$; $p < 0.01$) and academic adjustment dimension ($t = 2.50$; $p < 0.05$). The rest of the other dimensions like self pity, loneliness, health adjustment and social adjustment are statistically not significant.

It is observed that foreign students adjusted better on both emotionality and academic adjustment dimensions than Indian students. Foreign students tend to feel more secured as they are provided facilities by the authorities of the campus such as counselling. They enjoy overseas scholarships from their respective countries. Especially for the students of Gulf region, their money would be multiplied in exchange of Indian money. The financial security and the authorities support may enhance the emotional adjustment for the foreign students. With regard to academic adjustment, foreign students, by virtue of being conversant with English language which benefited to comprehend the subject concepts in higher education. Whereas for Indian students, particularly in Andhra University region mother tongue in Telugu language. Based on language foreign students' academic adjustment was better than Indian students. Barrat and Huba (1994) supported the English language skills.

4. Comparison Across Permanent Place of Residence

The mean scores of personality dimensions in comparison across the permanent place of residence i.e., rural and urban are tabulated in the Table 4.4. (*See on next page*)

It can be observed that the academic adjustment dimension obtained the statistically significant value. Whereas the other dimensions like self-pity, loneliness, emotionality, health adjustment and social adjustment are not significant. More elaborately, the academic adjustment ($t = 3.19$; $p<0.01$) statistically significant in comparison across the permanent place of residence i.e., rural and urban hostel students.

The difference between the mean scores is less; even urban students got better academic adjustment than rural students. Urban students belong to the towns and cities of the local districts of the University. Most of the urban localities in this zone are well equipped with the good quality of schools. Their instruction and methods of teaching facilitate the students to receive good quality of education. Those facilities are less in rural regions and rural students were not competitive with urban students. M.M. Kasinath (1990) and Alexander and Packiam (1998) results of earlier studies are in consistent with these findings.

Table 4

Permanent Place of Residence and Personality

(N= 556)

Dimensions	*Mean & S.D.*	*Rural (N=283)*	*Urban (N=273)*	*t Values*
1. Self Pity	Mean	6.18	5.75	1.79
	S.D.	2.76	2.96	
2. Loneliness	Mean	1.46	1.47	0.10
	S.D.	1.07	1.15	
3. Emotionality	Mean	4.20	4.08	0.64
	S.D.	2.12	2.31	
4. Health Adjustment	Mean	3.01	2.78	1.54
	S.D.	1.67	1.78	
5. Academic Adjustment	Mean	3.48	3.05	3.19**
	S.D.	1.50	1.63	
6. Social Adjustment	Mean	3.95	3.69	1.40
	S.D.	2.19	2.09	

* P < 0.05.

** P < 0.01.

5. Comparison Across Previous Hostel Experience

The mean scores of the personality dimensions in comparison across previous hostel experience i.e., experience and no-experience of the hostel students is recorded in the Table 4.5.

Table 4.5

Previous Hostel Experience and Personality

(N= 556)

Dimensions	*Mean & S.D.*	*Experience (N=414)*	*No Experience (N=142)*	*t Values*
1. Self Pity	Mean	5.98	5.96	0.08
	S.D.	2.91	2.80	
2. Loneliness	Mean	1.43	1.53	0.98
	S.D.	1.11	1.11	
3. Emotionality	Mean	4.05	4.26	1.05
	S.D.	2.26	2.16	
4. Health Adjustment	Mean	2.89	2.90	0.00
	S.D.	1.77	1.68	
5. Academic Adjustment	Mean	3.28	3.26	0.17
	S.D.	1.62	1.51	
6. Social Adjustment	Mean	3.82	3.82	0.03
	S.D.	2.16	2.11	

* $P < 0.05$.

** $P < 0.01$.

It can be observed that the all personality adjustment dimensions are statistically not significant.

The table showed that there is no significant difference between the previous experience and no experience of hostel students in the dimensions of personality adjustment. The demographical variable of comparison across hostel experience and no-experience had not at all influence the personality adjustment. The values denote that the hostel experience would not effect the personality adjustment of hostel students.

6. Comparison across Faculties

One-way analysis of variance (ANOVA) tests were conducted for the five faculties i.e., Arts, Science, Engineering, Medical and Law Students on scores of the personality adjustment dimensions for obtaining the 'F' values. The means scores of the personality adjustment dimensions in comparison across faculties of Arts, Science, Engineering, Medical and Law hostel students are tabulated in Table 4.6.

Table 4.6

Faculty and Personality

(N= 556)

Dimension	*Mean & S.D.*	*Arts (N= 129)*	*Science (N=122)*	*Engg (N=105)*	*Medicine (N =100)*	*Law (N=100)*	*F values*
1. Self pity	Mean	6.32	6.20	6.10	5.14	5.93	2.89*
	S.D.	2.87	3.05	2.84	2.80	2.60	
2. Loneliness	Mean	1.62	1.55	1.52	1.15	1.46	2.92*
	S.D.	1.16	1.15	1.01	1.00	1.16	
3. Emotionality	Mean	4.48	4.13	4.15	3.66	4.48	1.94
	S.D.	2.51	2.09	2.09	2.02	2.25	
4. Health Adjustment	Mean	3.23	2.94	2.68	2.31	3.23	5.58**
	S.D.	1.86	1.61	1.63	1.62	1.74	
5. Academic Adjustment	Mean	3.31	3.19	3.55	3.03	3.28	1.50
	S.D.	1.76	1.60	1.37	1.57	1.50	
6. Social Adjustment	Mean	3.92	4.03	3.90	3.46	3.73	1.16
	S.D.	2.19	2.19	2.13	1.86	2.27	

* $P < 0.05$.

** $P < 0.01$.

The Table indicates that differences in personality adjustment dimensions like self-pity, loneliness, and health adjustments are statistically significant. T-tests were conducted to examine.

Students studying professional courses are better adjusted than students of the other faculties, especially with regard to the self-pity dimension. The frustrated feelings, disappointment feelings and sadness feelings are low in medical students. Such type of feelings would be raised for the maladjusted students. With regard to the arts students such type of maladjusted behaviour is more. In the career of a student, after successful completion of their respective courses, better placements for professional courses students like engineering, medicine and law. In case of science students also some better opportunities are reserved after completion of their courses. Whereas in arts students the opportunities are less, and at the same time due to the policies of the government like privatisation, contractual basis, the struggle for existence would be increased. Based on these reasons, the self-pity was more in arts students rather than other faculties' students.

With regard to the loneliness dimension also the students of medicine feel secured, whereas in arts students the feeling of isolation was more. This dimension was also like the previous dimension that the professional courses students adjusted better in loneliness. When the person feels depressed, he would like to spend lonely. The depressed moods, frustrated feelings are high in arts students due to lack of proper placements after completion of their courses. The majority of arts students are doing their courses, not based on their future plan are likely to experience loneliness.

Regarding health adjustment, the medical students were better, due to their familiarity in their health habits. In science and engineering students also the health adjustment was better. Whereas in arts and law students, the health adjustment was less in comparison with other faculties. Generally arts and law students, not familiar with the health habits, even if they know, they will not follow due to their negligence of health.

In all these three significant dimensions viz., self-pity, loneliness and health adjustments, medical students adjusted better in comparison with other faculties students. Arts students are low in these entire three dimensions in personality adjustment.

Mohan and Kaur's (1991) study is consistent with the above results, whereas S.S. Rajan, Ashrafullah and V.N. Rajan. (1988) Study some faculty differences were found in adjustment.

7. Comparison Across Present Hostel Experience in Years

One-way analysis of variance (ANOVA) tests were conducted for the scores of personality adjustment dimensions in comparison across present hostel experience in years i.e., one year, 2 years, 3 years, 4 years and 5 years for obtaining 'F' values. The mean scores are tabulated in the Table 4.7.

Table 4. 7

Present Hostel Experience and Personality

(N= 556)

Dimensions	*Mean & S.D.*	*1 year (N= 141)*	*2 years (N=132)*	*3 years (N=80)*	*4 years (N =119)*	*5 years (N=84)*	*F values*
1. Self pity	Mean	6.53	6.05	5.90	5.39	5.78	2.73*
	S.D.	3.16	2.57	2.77	2.73	2.94	
2. Loneliness	Mean	1.58	1.47	1.52	1.36	1.39	0.73
	S.D.	1.15	1.17	1.03	1.04	1.14	
3. Emotionality	Mean	4.45	4.22	3.75	3.99	4.07	1.52
	S.D.	2.39	2.22	2.24	1.94	2.24	
4. Health Adjustment	Mean	3.10	3.13	2.61	2.62	2.84	2.47*
	S.D.	1.84	1.67	1.60	1.69	1.75	
5. Academic Adjustment	Mean	3.48	3.27	2.91	3.26	3.28	1.70
	S.D.	1.67	1.56	1.54	1.33	1.78	
6. Social Adjustment	Mean	3.97	3.84	3.52	3.79	3.85	0.58
	S.D.	2.38	2.10	1.96	1.99	2.16	

* $P < 0.05$.

** $P < 0.01$.

The self pity and health adjustment dimensions are statistically significant in comparison across present hostel experience whereas the other dimensions like loneliness, emotionality, academic adjustment and social adjustment are not significant.

The personality scores of students with 3, 4 and 5 years of hostel experience were comparatively better than that of 1 and 2 year experience of hostel students in self pity dimension. As the experience increases in hotel the adjustment related to self-pity increases. One year and 2 years experience students are suffering more frustrated on self and pity on themselves. As the experience increases, the ability to cope up with self would be increased. In case of health adjustment also the same discussion would be applied.

The better adjustment would be observed in 3, 4 and 5 years experience students, whereas in one and 2 years experience students, the health adjustment was comparatively less. In this situation also the ability to cope with health adjustment will be increased in duration of time. This was happened because of the familiarity of the good health habits were observed by the students on duration of time. They would learn those habits one by one, when their experience increases in hostel. As a result, the later year students are better health adjustment than previous year's students.

8. Comparison Across Economic Status

One way analysis of variance (ANOVA) tests were conducted for the scores of personality adjustment dimensions in comparison across economic status i.e., Annual income below Rs. 10, 000/-, between Rs. 10,000/- to Rs. 25,000/-, between Rs. 25,000/- to Rs. 50,000/-, between Rs. 50,000/- to, Rs. 1,00,000 and 100,000/- above for obtaining 'F' values. The mean scores are tabulated in the Table 4.8. (*See on next page*)

All the personality adjustment dimensions are statistically significant in comparison across economic status.

Students with an annual income below Rs. 10,000/- are categorised as poor students. Students whose annual incomes ranged between Rs. 10, 000/- to Rs. 25,000/- between Rs. 25,000/- to Rs. 50,000/- and between Rs. 50,000/- to Rs. 1,00,000/- are belongs to middle class categories I, II and III respectively. Finally, rich students are those whose annual income exceeded above Rs. 1,00,000/-.

Table 4.8
Economic Status and Personality
(N=556)

Dimensions	*Mean & S.D.*	*Below Rs. 10,000 (N=138)*	*Rs.10,000 - 25,000 (N=104)*	*Rs. 25,000 -.50,000 (N=95)*	*Rs. 50,000 - 1,00,000 (N=96)*	*Rs.1, 00,000 above (N=123)*	*F values*
1. Self Pity	Mean	6.61	5.85	5.70	5.92	5.59	2.55*
	SD	2.77	2.90	2.69	2.91	2.97	
2. Loneliness	Mean	1.74	1.31	1.36	1.37	1.46	3.01*
	SD	1.13	1.05	1.21	0.99	1.11	
3. Emotionality	Mean	4.80	4.06	4.02	3.63	3.95	4.76**
	SD	2.32	2.47	1.94	1.94	2.14	
4. Health Adjustment	Mean	3.59	2.72	2.58	2.42	2.87	8.83**
	SD	1.59	1.69	1.54	1.85	1.74	
5. Academic Adjustment	Mean	3.78	3.29	3.37	3.15	2.69	8.27**
	SD	1.55	1.48	1.43	1.72	1.51	
6. Social Adjustment	Mean	4.60	3.57	3.53	3.32	3.77	7.00**
	SD	2.31	2.07	1.97	2.02	2.01	

* $P < 0.05$.

** $P < 0.01$.

The comparison of mean scores in Rs. 1,00,000/- and above annual income group was comparatively better than that of other income groups of hostel students in self-pity dimension. Generally self-pity was observed in the students of low self-security and low financial status students. The self-pity was more in the students of below Rs. 10,000/- as their annual income. Whereas the students of Rs. 1,00,000/- and above students are adjusted better because of their financial security.

The better adjustment was observed in the middle class I group of students whereas the poor and rich income group students' loneliness was comparatively high. The students of poor status feel lonely and not interested to mingle with other hostelmates because of their poor financial status. This was also found in rich and high-income group that they are not interested to mingle with the students of low financial status. The middle three groups of students are adjusted better than the poor and rich group students.

With regard to the emotionality dimension, the middle class III and rich students were adjusted better than the remaining groups' students were. The high income and rich group students fulfilled the desires of their educational career in financial aspects. The poor group students, due to lack of money, may not be satisfied with their unfulfilled needs. Due to this reason certain amount of emotionality would be increased in poor students. Therefore, the high income and rich group student are adjusted better than poor group students in emotionality.

Concerning the health adjustment dimension, the middle class III groups of students are adjusted better whereas the poor group of students are less adjusted. Health is related with psychological and physical aspects. The poor income students suffered with more psychological feelings in the earlier dimensions. This cause also inherited to the health aspect. The mean scores of the middle class I, II and rich groups are also differed slightly and these groups are also adjusted better next to middle class III group.

On the academic adjustment dimension, the rich group of students is adjusted better than all the groups. The poor group of students is less adjusted in all groups. The academic adjustment in university level depends to a large extent on the earlier studies of the students. The rich group students had an early experience of English medium convent studies in their primary, secondary level. Even in graduation also, they have obtained the quality education from either college teaching or by tuition's. Therefore, in the university education also they have more chances to get better adjustment in academic aspects. Whereas in poor students, they cannot afford to study in convent schools and language is also an important aspect in university education. So poor students came from government schools with Telugu medium background. These discussion explain the better adjustment chances are more for rich group students in academic aspects.

In the social adjustment dimension, the middle class III group of students adjusted better and the poor group of students less adjusted in social aspect. The group relations are dependent on the understanding of the individuals. However, some influence on spending for the basic utilities in student career. Due to financial problems poor students withdraw from the social aspects. The remaining groups are also adjusted better with small fluctuations. The reasons indicated that the financial aspects influence social adjustment of hostel students.

Overall, the high middle class group and rich students groups are better personality adjustments whereas the poor student group has poor personality adjustment. Therefore, the economic status of the students much influences the personality adjustment.

Khan (1991), Mohan and Kaur (1991), Miya and Krishna (1996) and Mishra and Singh (1998) earlier results of their studies are consistent with the results of personality adjustment. In all their studies there were significant differences between personality and adjustment of students.

Summary of the Findings Regarding Personality Factors

The objective of personality factors is to examine the personality of hostel students and the impact of individual factors on the personality. The hypothesis constructed for personality is the demographic variables will have a significant influence on personality.

The age group of below 25 years emotional adjustment was less than above 25 years students. Female students suffered with loneliness and emotionality in comparison with male counterparts. Foreign students adjusted better than Indian students in emotionality. Urban students adjusted better than rural students in academic adjustment. The previous hostel experience does not influence personality. In faculty studies professional students (medicine) adjusted better than non-professional students (arts). The students having more experience in hostel life adjusted better than the students having less experience. Middle class and above middle class students adjusted better than poor and lower middle class students in economic status.

The results regarding the interaction of individual variables had shown that urban students aged more than 25 years had more positive personality dimensions. This suggests that apart from the age of the hostel student their permanent place of residence is equally important. Further, girls from rural settings shoed better spiritual adjustment.

All the above-mentioned personality factors influence adjustment of students. Therefore, the above-mentioned hypothesis is consistent with the findings of personality factors. The hypothesis set for the present personality study is accepted.

SECTION – II

HOSTEL ENVIRONMENT ADJUSTMENT

The scores of each respective dimension of hostel environment are computed and tabulated for obtaining the values of 't' scores and 'F" scores. The mean scores measures the degree of adjustment in respective dimension. The high mean scores indicate the better adjustments of the hostel environment dimensions. The significant 't' values and 'F' values are discussed and the statistically not significant dimensions were neglected.

1. Comparison Across Age

The mean scores of the variables of hostel environment in comparison across age i.e., age below 25 years and age 25 years and above are tabulated in Table 4.9.

Table 4.9
Age and Hostel Environment Adjustment
(N= 556)

Dimensions	*Mean & S.D.*	*Age below 25 yr. (N=414)*	*Age 25yrs and above (N=142)*	*t Values*
1. Room	Mean	30.67	30.24	1.22
	S.D.	3.63	3.57	
2. Toilet	Mean	16.44	16.05	1.76
	S.D.	2.15	2.53	
3. Food & Dining Hall	Mean	4.13	4.05	0.75
	S.D.	1.05	1.10	
4. Hostelmates & Servants	Mean	21.35	21.02	0.83
	S.D.	4.18	3.70	
5. Health & Recreation	Mean	17.85	18.33	1.50
	S.D.	3.32	3.14	
6. Guest	Mean	9.41	9.28	0.56
	S.D.	2.35	2.45	
7. Information	Mean	10.09	10.13	0.13
	S.D.	2.81	2.54	
8. Crisis	Mean	6.99	7.45	2.12*
	S.D.	2.24	2.11	
9. Financial	Mean	21.93	21.71	0.63
	S.D.	3.54	3.44	
10. Spiritual	Mean	2.71	2.66	0.32
	S.D.	1.62	1.57	

* $P < 0.05$.

** $P < 0.01$.

The crisis dimension across the age groups is statistically significant.

In the elaborate description crisis dimension versus age below 25 years and age 25 years and above hostel students, the value is statistically significant ($t = 2.12; p<0.05$). The mean scores of age 25 years and above group students were adjusted better than age below 25 years hostel students in crisis dimension.

The results suggest that the crisis dimension included with room crisis and water crisis in hostel. Students aged above 25 years have a previous experience in these two aspects. They store water in room or wake up early for freshening up. They would like to hand over the room when the authorities asked. The long duration of stay in hostel develop some association between authorities and senior students. Those aspects make the high age group adjusted better. Whereas in age group of below 25 years, such type of measures would be developed in later years by way of experience. Those reasons indicate that the high age group students are better adjusted than below 25 years age group.

Mukhopadhyay et al., (1996) in their study explained that the normal hostel students' emotionality would be increased in their transition. Takahashi and Majima (1994) found that the age mate dominant students adjusted well than below 25 years age group. These studies support the results of the present study.

2. Comparison Across Sex

The mean scores of the variables of hostel environment in comparison across male and female hostel students are tabulated in Table 4.10. (*See on next page*)

The room adjustment, toilet, health and recreation, crisis and financial adjustments are statistically significant.

The room, toilet and financial adjustments female students mean scores are comparatively higher than male students indicates the better adjustment in these three dimensions than male students. Whereas the health and recreation and crisis dimensions male students are better adjusted than female students.

Table 4.10
Gender and Hostel Environment Adjustment
(N= 556)

Dimensions	*Mean & S.D.*	*Males (N=299)*	*Females (N=257)*	*t Values*
1. Room	Mean	30.08	31.12	3.42**
	S.D.	3.65	3.49	
2. Toilet	Mean	16.09	16.63	2.84**
	S.D.	2.49	1.92	
3. Food & Dining Hall	Mean	4.05	4.18	1.46
	S.D.	1.12	0.99	
4. Hostelmates & Servants	Mean	21.09	21.46	1.05
	S.D.	4.07	4.04	
5. Health & Recreation	Mean	18.29	17.61	2.46*
	S.D.	3.15	3.40	
6. Guest	Mean	9.29	9.48	0.94
	S.D.	2.33	2.43	
7. Information	Mean	10.05	10.17	0.51
	S.D.	2.75	2.75	
8. Crisis	Mean	7.43	6.73	3.72**
	S.D.	2.19	2.19	
9. Financial	Mean	21.18	22.69	5.16**
	S.D.	3.53	3.32	
10. Spiritual	Mean	2.72	2.66	0.46
	S.D.	1.60	1.63	

* $P < 0.05$.

** $P < 0.01$.

With regard to room adjustment it can be stated that female students spend most of the time in their rooms and hence the maintenance of their room is likely to be better. Male students due to some negligence or by spending most of the time outside, their room adjustment was less in comparison with female students.

The female students were adjusted better than male students with regard to toilet. This was happened because the time spent in bathrooms by female students is likely to be more comparable with males. They look after the cleanliness in bathrooms. This was not found incase of males.

With regard to the health and recreation dimension male students adjusted better. There are so many opportunities for maintain health and recreation for male students like attending Gym or doing exercise etc. whereas for female students, the less opportunities cause comparatively lower than male students.

Male students adjusted better than female students in crisis dimension. Male students overcome this factor by so many other aspects like, storing of water, utilising well water, collection from tanks, freshen in other hostels etc. whereas in female students such type of adjustments are lower than male students.

In financial adjustment female students are better adjusted. Generally male students spend more time outside; there was much chance to spend money for transport or for domestic purpose. Female students spend only for their domestic purpose and keep some amount for reserve. Therefore, in financial adjustment female students were adjusted better than male students.

3. Comparison Across Nationality

The mean scores of hostel environment dimensions in comparison across nationality i.e., foreign students and Indian students are tabulated in Table 4.11. (*See on next page*)

The dimensions of room, hostelmates and servant, guest, financial and spiritual adjustments in comparison across nationality are statistically significant.

Table 4.11
Nationality and Hostel Adjustment
(N= 556)

Dimensions	*Mean and S.D.*	*Foreign Students (N=40)*	*Indian Students (N=516)*	*t Values*
1. Room	Mean	29.07	30.68	2.72**
	S.D.	3.68	3.59	
2. Toilet	Mean	16.00	16.37	1.00
	S.D.	2.00	2.28	
3. Food and Dining Hall	Mean	3.80	4.13	1.94
	S.D.	1.28	1.04	
4. Hostelmates and Servants	Mean	18.80	21.45	4.03**
	S.D.	3.76	4.02	
5. Health and Recreation	Mean	18.15	17.96	0.33
	S.D.	2.44	3.34	
6. Guest	Mean	10.17	9.31	2.20*
	S.D.	2.06	2.39	
7. Information	Mean	10.17	10.10	0.16
	S.D.	2.90	2.74	
8. Crisis	Mean	7.55	7.07	1.30
	S.D.	2.03	2.23	
9. Financial	Mean	20.47	21.98	2.63**
	S.D.	3.79	3.47	
10. Spiritual	Mean	3.25	2.65	2.24*
	S.D.	1.51	1.61	

* $P < 0.05$.

** $P < 0.01$.

More specifically the room dimension ($t = 2.72$; $p<0.01$) Hostelmates and servants ($t = 4.03$; $p < 0.01$), Guest ($t = 2.20$; $p<0.05$), financial ($t = 2.63$; $p < 0.01$) and spiritual ($t = 2.24$; $p < 0.05$) hostel adjustments are significant in comparison across nationality of hostel students. The variations of mean scores were slightly differing in both the groups. However Indian students' adjustment was better in room, hostelmates and servants and financial dimensions than foreign students. Whereas foreign students were better adjustment in guest and spiritual adjustment than Indian students.

In room adjustment discussion, foreign students governed by the University authorities and their resident rooms are located outside the campus and they were self-financed. However, in the case of Indian students, University campus based hostels with provision of mess halls. Due to the less difficulty of room, Indian students adjusted better than foreign students.

In hostelmates and servants dimension, foreign students make their own arrangements of food by themselves without dependence on servants. If they want servants, they have to bear the expenses for servants. Whereas Indian students, their work was much easier with hostel servants. Therefore, they make to work with servants and maintain cordial relationships with other hostelmates. Due to these reasons Indian students are adjusted better than foreign students.

With regard to the guest dimension, foreign students were adjusted better than Indian students. For guest, it was a problem for the Indian students for providing food or shelter because, such type of facilities was not found in the rules and regulations of the hostel. Whereas in case of foreign students, since their hostel rooms were self-financed, so there was a chance of guest adjustment for foreign students.

In financial adjustment, Indian students were better adjusted than foreign students. Generally foreign students spend for their needs without hesitating. They won't bother for money in fulfilling their needs. Whereas Indian students, reduce the spending of amounts by restricting some needs. They keep some amounts in reserve for future needs of urgency. These cultural habits evaluate better adjustment for Indian students than foreign students.

Related to spiritual dimension, foreign students' adjustment was better than Indian students. Most of the foreign students in the campus came from the religions of Islam, Buddhist and Christianity. They won't criticise other ritual practices. Whereas Indian students came from the mixed religions, also includes the atheists not believe in religion. Due to those reasons, foreign students' adjustments are better than Indian students in spiritual dimension. Tabacyk and Driggers (1989) supported this religious belief on personality adjustment.

4. Comparison Across Permanent Place of Residence

The mean scores of hostel environment dimensions in comparison across place of residence of students are tabulated in Table 4.12. (*See on next page*)

Table 4.12 provided results of the influence of the permanent place of residence on hostel environment adjustment.

Rural and urban students differ significantly on the dimensions of crisis ($t = 3.62$; $p<0.01$) and spiritual adjustment ($t = 5.26$; $p<0.01$). The urban students' adjustment in these two dimensions was better than rural students.

With regard to 'Crisis' urban students are more likely to be familiar with water crisis, so that such type of scarcity is common in towns and cities. Due to these sociological aspects, the students act according to the scarcity of water in hostels. For room also, they do not hesitate to report to the authorities. Whereas in rural students due to lack of experience their adjustment was slightly reduced compared to urban students. In case of room also, they feel insecure while dealing with the authorities.

In spiritual adjustment also, urban student's beliefs were more than rural students. They won't criticize other religion practices. The respect of other religions was more in urban students. Due to these reasons, urban students adjusted better than rural students in spiritual adjustment.

Kasinath (1990) and Alexander and Packiam (1998) results of earlier studies are inconsistent with these findings.

Table 4.12

Permanent Place of Residence and Hostel Environment Adjustment

(N= 556)

Dimensions	*Mean and S.D.*	*Rural (N=283)*	*Urban (N=273)*	*t Values*
1. Room	Mean	30.50	30.63	0.40
	S.D.	3.46	3.77	
2. Toilet	Mean	16.18	16.50	1.67
	S.D.	2.46	2.03	
3. Food and Dining Hall	Mean	4.05	4.17	1.39
	S.D.	1.07	1.05	
4. Hostelmates and Servants	Mean	21.16	21.36	0.59
	S.D.	3.83	4.29	
5. Health and Recreation	Mean	18.22	17.72	1.79
	S.D.	3.35	3.20	
6. Guest	Mean	9.21	9.54	1.62
	S.D.	2.52	2.20	
7. Information	Mean	9.89	10.32	1.88
	S.D.	2.64	2.84	
8. Crisis	Mean	6.77	7.45	3.62**
	S.D.	2.32	2.05	
9. Financial	Mean	21.78	21.98	0.67
	S.D.	3.41	3.62	
10. Spiritual	Mean	2.35	3.05	5.26**
	S.D.	1.54	1.60	

* $P < 0.05$.

** $P < 0.01$.

5. Comparison Across Previous Hostel Experience

The mean scores of the hostel adjustment dimensions in comparison across previous hostel experience and inexperience are tabulated in Table 4.13.

Table 4.13
Previous Hostel Experience and Hostel Environment Adjustment
(N= 556)

Dimensions	*Mean and S.D.*	*Experience (N=326)*	*No Experience (N=230)*	*t Values*
1. Room	Mean	30.45	30.72	0.87
	S.D.	3.69	3.51	
2. Toilet	Mean	16.28	16.43	0.74
	S.D.	2.46	1.95	
3. Food and Dining Hall	Mean	4.01	4.25	2.55*
	S.D.	1.09	1.01	
4. Hostelmates & Servants	Mean	21.07	21.53	1.33
	S.D.	4.06	4.05	
5. Health and Recreation	Mean	18.12	17.76	1.26
	S.D.	3.12	3.50	
6. Guest	Mean	9.24	9.56	1.54
	S.D.	2.34	2.41	
7. Information	Mean	10.27	9.86	1.76
	S.D.	2.77	2.69	
8. Crisis	Mean	7.01	7.24	1.19
	S.D.	2.18	2.27	
9. Financial	Mean	21.61	22.24	2.07*
	S.D.	3.54	3.45	
10. Spiritual	Mean	2.77	2.59	1.27
	S.D.	1.63	1.58	

* $P < 0.05$.

** $P < 0.01$.

The hostel adjustment dimension food and dinning hall and financial adjustment are statistically significant.

The food and dinning hall adjustment (t = 2.55; $p<0.05$) and financial adjustment (t = 2.07; $p<0.05$) are statistically significant across the previous hostel experience and inexperience students. In both dimensions, the variations are slightly, but the inexperience students adjusted better than experience students.

With regard to food and dinning hall adjustment, students with no prior experience, by way of newness and by observing the things in the mess take their food to satisfaction. The noise of the mess would not affect their taking of food. Whereas experienced students, due to some negligence of centralisation do not show that much interest in taking of food.

In financial adjustment also, students with no prior experience adjusted better than students with experience. Due to some fear of newness in hostel, the students keep some amount in reserve and reduce the unnecessary spending. But the experienced students act according to their moods and needs. This cause makes the no experience students adjusted better than experience students.

6. Comparison across Faculties

The results regarding the influence of faculty on the mean scores of the hostel environment adjustment are tabulated in Table 4.14. (*See on next page*)

The hostel adjustment dimensions like room, toilet, food and dinning hall, hostelmates and servants, health and recreation, information, crisis, financial and spiritual adjustments are statistically significant. One-way analysis of various (ANOVA) tests was conducted for obtained the value of 'F'.

In room dimension, medical students adjusted better than other faculties. The attachments with the roommates, utilising the furniture properly in room, maintenance of the room, all these aspects are better in medical students. The course itself was a dignified course so that the students maintaining the same aspects. The room adjustment for other faculties was more or less equal. For the second dimension 'toilet' also medical student's adjustment

Table 4.14

Faculty and Hostel Environment Adjustment

(N= 556)

Dimensions	*Mean and S.D.*	*Arts (N= 129)*	*Science (N=122)*	*Engg. (N=105)*	*Medicine (N =100)*	*Law (N=100)*	*F values*
1. Room	Mean	30.25	30.15	30.87	31.43	30.28	2.42*
	S.D.	3.76	3.35	3.98	3.33	3.49	
2. Toilet	Mean	16.06	16.03	16.50	17.17	16.09	4.95**
	S.D.	2.27	2.18	1.84	2.07	2.71	
3. Food and Dining Hall	Mean	3.86	4.10	4.27	4.47	3.92	6.14**
	S.D.	1.14	1.05	0.98	0.82	1.16	
4. Hostelmates and Servants	Mean	21.16	20.65	22.42	21.47	20.72	3.43**
	S.D.	4.34	3.66	4.12	4.37	3.55	
5. Health and Recreation	Mean	17.89	18.73	17.31	17.92	17.92	2.76**
	S.D.	4.01	2.98	2.91	2.68	3.38	

(Contd...)

Dimensions	*Mean and S.D.*	*Arts (N= 129)*	*Science (N=122)*	*Engg. (N=105)*	*Medicine (N =100)*	*Law (N=100)*	*F values*
6. Guest	Mean	9.11	9.50	9.50	9.65	9.17	1.06
	S.D.	2.18	1.84	2.72	2.76	2.39	
7. Information	Mean	9.41	10.61	10.23	10.17	10.17	3.19*
	S.D.	2.58	2.94	2.60	2.86	2.62	
8. Crisis	Mean	6.31	7.30	7.70	7.69	6.69	9.33**
	S.D.	2.23	2.14	2.18	2.03	2.15	
9. Financial	Mean	21.17	22.26	22.15	22.56	21.36	3.36**
	S.D.	3.19	3.78	3.38	3.54	3.52	
10. Spiritual	Mean	2.53	2.53	3.20	3.24	2.05	10.71**
	S.D.	1.65	1.59	1.54	1.57	1.38	

* $P < 0.05$.

** $P < 0.01$.

was better than all the groups. Medical students utilise the sanitary ware, bathrooms in a clean manner comparatively with other faculty students. Next to the medical students, the other faculty students are almost equal in their toilet adjustment.

In case of food and dining hall adjustment, medical students mean score was high indicating that, even if the noises were more in the mess, they took food to their satisfaction. Such type of adjustment was little bit low in arts and law students because of less patience science and engineering students are adjusted better than arts and law students in food and dining hall adjustment.

In hostelmates and servants dimension engineering students are better than all groups of students. Maintaining friendly relationships with the hostelmates at the same time maintaining the hostel servants to work for them was better in engineering students. Medical and arts students are adjusted better than science and law students in hostelmates and servants dimension.

With regard to health and recreation dimension, science students were better adjusted comparatively with all five groups of students. As a science faculty, students maintaining clean habits, good health habits and proper physical exercise. Actually medical students know all these facts but the busy schedules of the study not cooperative to maintain better health and recreation. The adjustments of other faculties were almost equal in health and recreation dimension.

Related to information dimension science students were adjusted better. Observing the notice board and communicate with hostel mess authorities by applying heave application in case of ill health or to look for any work, such type of activities observed in science students. Whereas due to carelessness that was less in arts students. In engineering, medicine and law faculties the information adjustment was almost equal.

Only the Crisis adjustment also the professional courses students were adjusted better than arts and science students. They utilise the water properly when there was a scarcity, when the authorities demand to vacate the room, they would obey to handover it. Whereas in arts and science students such types of activities are less in crisis adjustment.

In financial adjustment science, engineering and medical students were adjusted better than arts and law students. The proper utilisation of money and kept some amount in reserve for the needs of urgency, were the habits of better-adjusted students. Those activities are less in arts and law students.

In case of spiritual adjustment engineering and medical students were adjusted better, whereas in law students, it was less, criticise others religious aspects were not found in the students of engineering and medical students. In law students the spiritual adjustment was less in comparing with other faculties. This was likely because of their profession, that not to believe those abstract things. In arts and science students the spiritual adjustments are equal.

Mohan and Kaur's (1991) study is consistent with the above results, whereas in Rajan, Asrafullah and Rajan's (1998) study, some faculty differences were found in adjustment.

7. Comparison Across Present Hostel Experience

The mean scores of the hostel adjustment dimensions in comparison across present hostel experience i.e., 1 year, 2 years, 3 years, 4 years and 5 years are tabulated in Table 4.15. (*See on next page*)

One-way Analysis of variance (ANOVA) tests were conducted for the scores for obtaining 'F' values. The hotel adjustment dimensions like toilet, hostelmates and servants, crisis and spiritual adjustment are statistically significant across present hostel experience.

With regard to toilet adjustment, 4 years experience student adjusted better. The observed facts of the table indicate that as the experience increases, the level of adjustment also increases. The common reason for this fact was, the senior students were familiar for the situation of toilet adjustment in hostel, where as in 5 years students the toilet adjustment was less comparatively with 3 years and 4 years experienced students.

Table 4.15

Present Hostel Experience and Hostel Environment Adjustment

(N= 556)

Dimensions	*Mean and S.D.*	*1 year (N= 141)*	*2 years (N=132)*	*3 years (N=80)*	*4 years (N =119)*	*5 years (N=84)*	*F Values*
1. Room	Mean	30.48	30.12	30.30	31.20	30.76	1.61
	S.D.	3.37	3.79	3.91	3.48	3.57	
2. Toilet	Mean	15.98	15.94	16.78	16.92	16.33	4.73**
	S.D.	2.34	2.23	2.21	1.93	2.46	
3. Food & Dining Hall	Mean	4.09	3.96	4.06	4.28	4.17	1.50
	S.D.	1.03	1.10	1.24	0.97	0.99	
4. Hostelmates and Servants	Mean	21.51	20.80	20.55	22.26	20.84	3.26*
	S.D.	3.81	4.26	3.89	4.24	3.82	
5. Health and Recreation	Mean	18.01	17.73	17.88	18.14	18.16	0.34
	S.D.	3.73	3.25	3.55	2.81	2.90	

(Contd...)

Dimensions	*Mean and S.D.*	*1 year (N= 141)*	*2 years (N=132)*	*3 years (N=80)*	*4 years (N =119)*	*5 years (N=84)*	*F Values*
6. Guest	Mean	9.43	9.25	8.83	9.68	9.57	1.78
	S.D.	2.08	2.28	2.56	2.67	2.32	
7. Information	Mean	10.19	9.82	9.80	10.05	10.77	1.88
	S.D.	2.72	2.68	2.80	2.60	2.97	
8. Crisis	Mean	6.78	6.78	6.61	7.60	7.94	7.18**
	S.D.	2.24	2.26	2.23	2.15	1.83	
9. Financial	Mean	21.91	21.46	21.37	22.10	22.64	1.99
	S.D.	3.54	3.22	3.85	3.41	3.64	
10. Spiritual	Mean	2.34	2.70	2.41	3.21	2.82	5.67**
	S.D.	1.64	1.56	1.50	1.56	1.62	

* $P < 0.05$.

** $P < 0.01$.

For the dimension of hostelmates and servants, four years experience students adjusted better than other groups. Generally majority of engineering and medical students were present in the 4 years seniority group because that was the last year of their study. This group maintains good relationships with other hostelmates and at the same time they would control the servants to work in a proper manner. One-year experience students adjusted better than 2 years, 3 years and 5 years students. This was happened because of early enthusiasm and novelty, one-year experience students maintain good relationships with elders 2 years, 3 years and 5 years experience students' adjustments in hostelmates and servant dimension are almost equal.

On the crisis dimension, 5 years experience students adjusted better than other groups. Next position by 4 years experienced students. Mainly the reason was the lot of experience about the crisis factor and known aspects of overcome from crisis. So better adjustment in water crisis and room crisis aspects for the 5 years and 4 years experience students. 3 years experience students are low in adjustment of crisis whereas one year and 2 years experience students, the crisis adjustment was equal.

In the dimension of spiritual adjustment, 4 years experience students adjusted better when compared with one-year experience students. Due to experience and duration of time the criticism about ritual of others was less in experienced students, whereas due to inexperience the criticisms are more in one year experienced students. 5 years and 2 years experienced students are better than 3 years experience students in spiritual adjustment dimension.

Over all 4 years and 5 years experience students i.e., senior students are better adjusted than 1 year 2 years and 3 years experience students in all the areas of hostel adjustment dimension

8. Comparison Across Economic Status

The mean scores of the hostel adjustment dimensions in comparison across economic status i.e., below Rs. 10,000/-, between Rs. 10,000/- to Rs. 25,000/-, between Rs. 25,000/- to Rs. 50,000/-, between Rs. 50,000/- to Rs. 1,00,000/- and Rs. 1,00,000/- and above hostel students are tabulated in Table 4.16.

Table 4.16

Economic Status and Hostel Environment Adjustment

(N=556)

Dimensions	*Mean and S.D.*	*Below Rs.10,000 (N=138)*	*Rs. 10,000-25,000 (N=104)*	*Rs. 25,000-50,000 (N=95)*	*Rs. 50,000-1,00,000 (N=96)*	*Rs. 1,00,000 above (N=123)*	*F Values*
1. Room	Mean	30.03	30.72	30.85	31.55	30.04	3.42**
	SD	3.74	3.29	3.22	3.48	3.96	
2. Toilet	Mean	15.83	16.29	16.27	16.88	16.59	3.59**
	SD	2.76	2.35	1.87	1.82	2.05	
3. Food and Dining Hall	Mean	3.92	4.12	4.04	4.34	4.20	2.60*
	SD	1.15	1.05	1.11	1.02	0.94	
4. Hostelmates and Servants	Mean	21.06	20.80	20.96	22.32	21.28	2.18
	SD	3.77	3.98	3.93	4.23	4.31	
5. Health and Recreation	Mean	17.92	17.98	17.78	18.28	17.95	0.29
	SD	3.41	3.75	3.18	2.86	3.14	

(Contd...)

Dimensions	*Mean and S.D.*	*Below Rs.10,000 (N=138)*	*Rs. 10,000-25,000 (N=104)*	*Rs. 25,000-50,000 (N=95)*	*Rs. 50,000-1,00,000 (N=96)*	*Rs. 1,00,000 above (N=123)*	*F Values*
6. Guest	Mean	8.92	9.19	9.13	9.83	9.88	4.04**
	SD	2.31	2.35	1.97	2.14	2.77	
7. information	Mean	9.73	10.33	9.94	10.33	10.27	1.18
	SD	2.79	2.63	2.59	2.74	2.89	
8. Crisis	Mean	6.47	6.83	7.08	7.76	7.56	6.90**
	SD	2.23	2.32	2.30	1.79	2.15	
9. Financial	Mean	21.07	21.25	22.84	22.14	22.35	5.26**
	SD	3.47	3.32	2.94	3.60	3.81	
10. Spiritual	Mean	2.00	2.68	2.58	2.95	3.37	13.54**
	SD	1.31	1.52	1.72	1.69	1.53	

* $P < 0.05$.

** $P < 0.01$.

One-way analysis of variance (ANOVA) tests were conducted for the scores for obtaining 'F' values. The hostel adjustment dimensions like room, toilet, food and dining hall, guest, crisis, financial and spiritual adjustments are statistically significant across economic status of the students.

In the room adjustment dimension the middle class III group of students adjusted better than all the groups. The middle class I and II group of students adjusted better than poor and rich students. The middle class group students got previous training in their homes related to handling of the furniture, electrical appliances and relationships with friends. Therefore, they are adjusted better in room adjustment. The poor students have not previous training and the rich group of students due to negligence in handling the things less adjusted than middle class students in room adjustment.

With regard to toilet adjustment the middle class III group students adjusted better. Next the rich group and the other middle class groups adjusted better than poor students. The parents from childhood level learns the sanitary toilet training. However, in nowadays every middle class family uses the sanitary appliances. Therefore, the previous home training helps the rich and middle class students to adjust better in toilets. Due to poverty the facilities are less in poor students.

Regarding food and dining hall adjustment the middle class III group adjusted better in all groups. Generally the financial status of the middle class students fluctuates. Sometimes they are suffered with low economy. Due to the experiences in economic aspects, they are adjusted well in food and dining hall.

In the adjustment of guest, rich students are adjusted better in all groups. The middle class III group also adjusted better. The high economic group students can afford their guests by providing shelter or food outside the campus by spending their money. Whereas the other group students have not that much sound to provide those aspects for their guests. Therefore, the high financial students got better adjustment in guest adjustment.

The middle class III group students adjusted better in crisis. Middle class students have an earlier experience of water scarcity in their places. Therefore, the high financial status groups adjusted for the crisis related to room or water because of their earlier experiences. The rich and middle class II group students are also adjusted better in this crisis.

With regard to financial adjustment, the middle class II group students adjusted better. The middle class II group students exactly in the middle of the financial status. They will know the value of money and how to utilise the money for their needs. Therefore, they are well adjusted in financial adjustments. The high income group students are also adjusted better in this dimension.

On the spiritual adjustment, the rich group of students adjusted better than all groups. Generally the people believe that God gives the riches. Therefore, they are spiritually adjusted. The middle class groups are adjusted better than poor students.

Overall, the results suggest that the high-income groups adjusted better in hostel adjustment dimensions. The economic status of the students influences the hostel adjustment of students.

Khan (1991), Mohan and Kaur (1991), Miya and Krishna (1996) and Mishra and Singh (1998) earlier results of their studies are consistent with the results of adjustment.

Summary of the Findings Regarding Hostel Environmental Factors

The objective of hostel environmental adjustment is to examine the hostel environmental adjustment of students and the impact of individual factors on hostel environmental adjustment. The hypothesis constructed for hostel environment adjustment is the demographic variables will have a significant influence on hostel environmental adjustment.

The findings reveal that students of 25 years and above adjusted better in crisis than below 25 years students. Female students adjusted better than male students in majority of hostel environmental adjustment factors. Foreign students adjusted better in guest and spiritual adjustment dimensions, whereas Indian students adjusted better in room, hostelmates and servants and financial adjustments. Urban students adjusted better than rural students in crisis and spiritual adjustments. The students having no experience previously in hostel adjusted better than experienced students in food and dining hall and financial adjustments. Professional students adjusted better than non-professional students in hostel environmental adjustment. The students having more experience in hostel adjusted better than the less experienced students in hostel environmental adjustment. Middle class and above class students adjusted better than poor and lower middle class students.

All the above-mentioned environmental factors influence adjustment of students. Therefore, the above-mentioned hypothesis is consistent with the findings of environmental factors. The hypothesis set for the present hostel environmental adjustment study is validated. So that the hypothesis is accepted.

SECTION - III

INTERACTION EFFECT

This section includes the results regarding the interaction of individual variables like age, gender and place of residence on personality and hostel environmental factors. This section was sub categorised in to three parts. First part included with the interaction of age and gender on personality and hostel environmental factors. Second part consists of the interaction of age and place of residence and the third part consists of the interaction of gender and place of residence on personality and hostel environmental factors.

The individual factor age was categorised into below 25 years and 25 years and above, gender includes the categorisation of male and female and the place of residence was categorised into rural and urban background students.

The personality scores measures the degree of maladjustment in hostel students. The higher mean scores indicate the degree of maladjustment in the respective dimensions.

Whereas the hostel environmental scores measures the degree of adjustment in hostel students. Higher means scores indicate the degree of adjustment in the respective dimensions.

1. Interaction of Age and Gender

The preliminary analysis of the data involved the interaction of the age and gender on personality factors. The means scores and F values are tabulated in Table 4.17.

Table 4.17

Interaction of Age and Gender on Personality Factors

Age		*>25 Years*		*< 25 years*		
Gender / *Dimensions*		*Male (n=192)*	*Female (n=222)*	*Male (n=107)*	*Female (n=35)*	*F value*
Self-pity	Mean	5.98	6.14	5.40	6.54	2.45
	S.D.	2.92	2.91	2.73	2.54	
Loneliness	Mean	1.37	1.57	1.32	1.91	2.66
	S.D.	1.01	1.18	1.12	1.12	
Emotionality	Mean	3.99	4.49	3.63	4.37	0.25
	S.D.	2.23	2.08	2.42	2.13	
Health adjustment	Mean	2.87	2.82	3.17	2.66	1.54
	S.D.	1.68	1.84	1.64	1.55	
Academic adjustment	Mean	3.42	3.08	3.40	3.31	0.49
	S.D.	1.64	1.44	1.77	1.43	
Social adjustment	Mean	3.82	3.82	3.80	3.97	0.12
	S.D.	2.06	2.07	2.36	2.47	

* P < 0.05.

** P < 0.01.

Table 4.17 shows no significant influence of the interaction of age and gender of the student was observed on their personality.

Table 4.18 shows the interaction of age and gender on hostel environmental factors.

Table 4.18

Interaction of Age and Gender on Hostel Environmental Factors

Age		*>25 Years*		*< 25 years*		
Gender		*Male*	*Female*	*Male*	*Female*	*F*
Dimensions		*(n=192)*	*(n=222)*	*(n=107)*	*(n=35)*	*value*
ROOM	Mean	30.08	31.19	30.08	30.74	0.33
	S.D.	3.74	3.47	3.53	3.71	
TOILET	Mean	16.34	16.54	15.65	17.29	8.64*
	S.D.	2.42	1.91	2.58	1.96	
FOOD AND DINING HALL	Mean	4.10	4.17	3.97	4.31	1.39
	S.D.	1.10	1.02	1.18	0.80	
HOSTELMATES AND SERVANTS	Mean	21.20	21.48	20.91	21.37	0.05
	S.D.	4.28	4.10	3.70	3.73	
HEALTH AND RECREATION	Mean	18.18	17.58	18.50	17.83	0.01
	S.D.	3.12	3.49	3.23	2.88	
GUEST	Mean	9.36	9.46	9.17	9.63	0.48
	S.D.	2.24	2.46	2.50	2.30	
INFORMATION	Mean	9.98	10.19	10.17	10.03	0.34
	S.D.	2.87	2.78	2.54	2.60	
CRISIS	Mean	7.55	6.51	7.21	8.17	17.95**
	S.D.	2.25	2.14	2.09	2.04	
FINANCIAL ADJUSTMENT	Mean	21.07	22.68	21.38	22.74	0.12
	S.D.	3.54	3.38	3.53	2.95	
SPIRITUAL ADJUSTMENT	Mean	2.83	2.61	2.54	3.03	4.08*
	S.D.	1.65	1.60	1.49	1.79	

* P < 0.05.

** P < 0.01.

It can be observed that all the personality dimensions are statistically insignificant.

A significant influence of the interaction of age and gender of the student has been observed with regard to their evaluation of the hostel environment. Significant influence was observed with regard to the toilet, crisis and spiritual dimensions. More specifically, it is observed that girls aged above 25 years showed better adjusted to these dimensions than the other groups.

2. Interaction of Age and Place of Residence

The mean scores of the interaction of age and place of residence on personality factors are tabulated in Table 4.19.

Table 4.19

Interaction of Age and Place of Residence on Personality Factors

Age		*>25 Years*		*< 25 years*		
Place of residence		*Rural*	*Urban*	*Rural*	*Urban*	*F*
Dimensions		*(n=207)*	*(n=207)*	*(n=76)*	*(n=66)*	*value*
Self-pity	Mean	6.19	5.95	6.17	5.12	2.11
	S.D.	2.84	2.99	2.54	2.84	
Loneliness	Mean	1.53	1.42	1.30	1.65	4.39*
	S.D.	1.07	1.13	1.06	1.22	
Emotionality	Mean	4.21	4.29	4.17	3.41	3.84*
	S.D.	1.98	2.33	2.49	2.16	
Health adjustment	Mean	2.90	2.80	3.32	2.74	1.96
	S.D.	1.70	1.83	1.57	1.65	
Academic adjustment	Mean	3.36	3.12	3.83	2.86	5.72*
	S.D.	1.48	1.60	1.53	1.74	
Social adjustment	Mean	3.86	3.78	4.21	3.42	2.93
	S.D.	2.12	2.00	2.35	2.35	

* $P < 0.05$.

** $P < 0.01$.

The dimensions of loneliness (F=4.40; P<0.05), emotionality (F=3.84; P<0.05) and academic adjustment (F=5.72; P<0.05) are statistically significant.

Table 4.19 indicates that urban students aged above 25 years showed better adjustment than the other groups with regard to personality dimensions like loneliness, emotional and academic adjustment.

The interactions of mean scores of age and place of residence on hostel environmental factors are tabulated in Table 4.20.

Table 4.20

Interaction of Age and Place of Residence on Hostel Environmental Factors

Age		*>25 Years*		*< 25 years*		
Place of residence		*Rural*	*Urban*	*Rural*	*Urban*	*F*
Dimensions		*(n=207)*	*(n=207)*	*(n=76)*	*(n=66)*	*value*
ROOM	Mean	30.74	30.61	29.86	30.70	1.92
	S.D.	3.44	3.82	3.49	3.63	
TOILET	Mean	16.42	16.47	15.55	16.64	5.59*
	S.D.	2.33	1.98	2.70	2.22	
FOOD AND DINING HALL	Mean	4.11	4.16	3.89	4.24	2.07
	S.D.	1.02	1.10	1.23	0.91	
HOSTELMATES AND SERVANTS	Mean	21.34	21.36	20.70	21.39	0.72
	S.D.	3.88	4.47	3.68	3.72	
HEALTH AND RECREATION	Mean	18.18	17.53	18.34	18.33	1.01
	S.D.	3.42	3.22	3.20	3.11	
GUEST	Mean	9.26	9.57	9.12	9.47	0.01
	S.D.	2.45	2.26	2.76	2.05	

(Contd...)

Age		>25 Years		< 25 years		
Place of residence		Rural	Urban	Rural	Urban	F
Dimensions		(n=207)	(n=207)	(n=76)	(n=66)	value
INFORMATION	Mean	9.95	10.25	9.74	10.59	1.07
	S.D.	2.77	2.87	2.26	2.78	
CRISIS	Mean	6.62	7.36	7.20	7.74	0.21
	S.D.	2.37	2.07	2.18	2.00	
FINANCIAL ADJUSTMENT	Mean	21.98	21.89	21.24	22.27	2.71
	S.D.	3.41	3.69	3.39	3.44	
SPIRITUAL ADJUSTMENT	Mean	2.37	3.06	2.32	3.06	0.03
	S.D.	1.58	1.61	1.47	1.62	

* P < 0.05.

** P < 0.01.

The toilet adjustment (F=5.58; P<0.05) only statistically significant.

Table 4.20 shows the interaction of age and place of residence on hostel environmental factors. With regard to the hostel dimensions, it is observed that urban students aged above 25 years showed better adjustment with regard to the hostel dimension of toilet.

3. Interaction of Gender and Place of Residence

The mean scores of interaction of gender and place of residence on personality factors are tabulated in Table 4.21.

The only dimension, emotionality (F=6.05; P<0.05) was statistically significant.

A significant influence of the interaction of sex and place of the student on their personality and adjustment to hostel environment is noted in Table 4.21.

Table 4.21
Interaction of Gender and Place of Residence on Personality Factors

Gender		*Male*		*Female*		
Place of residence		*Rural*	*Urban*	*Rural*	*Urban*	*F*
Dimensions		*(n=177)*	*(n=122)*	*(n=106)*	*(n=151)*	*value*
Self-pity	Mean	5.94	5.54	6.60	5.92	0.34
	S.D.	2.72	3.06	2.80	2.88	
Loneliness	Mean	1.42	1.24	1.55	1.66	2.44
	S.D.	1.03	1.08	1.16	1.19	
Emotionality	Mean	4.14	3.47	4.31	4.58	6.06*
	S.D.	2.29	2.28	1.83	2.24	
Health adjustment	Mean	3.07	2.85	2.91	2.73	0.02
	S.D.	1.65	1.70	1.73	1.85	
Academic adjustment	Mean	3.59	3.15	3.30	2.99	0.23
	S.D.	1.56	1.83	1.39	1.47	
Social adjustment	Mean	3.90	3.69	4.03	3.71	0.07
	S.D.	2.25	2.19	2.26	2.02	

* $P < 0.05$.

** $P < 0.01$.

The mean scores of interaction gender and place of residence on hostel environmental factors are tabulated in Table 4.22.

Table 4. 22
Interaction of Gender and Place of Residence on Hostel Environmental Factors

Gender		*MALE*		*FEMALE*		
Place of residence		*RURAL*	*URBAN*	*RURAL*	*URBAN*	*F*
Dimensions		*(n=177)*	*(n=122)*	*(n=106)*	*(n=151)*	*value*
ROOM	Mean	29.98	30.23	31.38	30.95	1.17
	S.D.	3.69	3.61	2.87	3.88	
TOILET	Mean	15.94	16.32	16.60	16.66	0.69
	S.D.	2.70	2.15	1.94	1.93	
FOOD AND DINING HALL	Mean	4.03	4.08	4.08	4.26	0.46
	S.D.	1.11	1.15	1.03	0.96	
HOSTELMATES AND SERVANTS	Mean	21.29	20.82	20.96	21.81	3.54*
	S.D.	3.88	4.36	3.77	4.20	
HEALTH AND RECREATION	Mean	18.40	18.15	17.93	17.38	0.27
	S.D.	3.34	2.87	3.37	3.42	
GUEST	Mean	9.08	9.60	9.45	9.50	1.30
	S.D.	2.31	2.33	2.85	2.10	
INFORMATION	Mean	9.90	10.27	9.88	10.38	0.07
	S.D.	2.59	2.97	2.74	2.75	
CRISIS	Mean	7.22	7.74	6.04	7.23	3.23
	S.D.	2.26	2.08	2.26	2.01	
FINANCIAL ADJUSTMENT	Mean	21.07	21.34	22.96	22.50	1.47
	S.D.	3.54	3.55	2.84	3.62	
SPIRITUAL ADJUSTMENT	Mean	2.59	2.93	1.96	3.16	9.87*
	S.D.	1.57	1.64	1.44	1.58	

* $P < 0.05$.

** $P < 0.01$.

The hostelmates and servants (F=3.54; P<0.05) and spiritual adjustment (F=9.87; P<0.05) dimensions are statistically significant.

Table 4.22 shows the interaction of gender and place of residence on hostel environmental factors. More specifically it is observed that urban boys showed better emotional and spiritual adjustment than the other groups of girls.

Summary of Findings with Regard to Interaction Effects

The results showed that female students aged 25 years and above adjusted in toilet and crisis dimensions. The urban students aged below 25 years adjusted better in loneliness and 25 years and above students adjusted better in emotionality, health adjustment and toilet adjustment. The urban male students adjusted better in emotionality whereas the female students adjusted better in hostelmates and servants and spiritual adjustment factors.

Boys aged above 25 and those from urban backgrounds showed better adjustment to the physical aspects of the hostel environment. Further, urban students aged above 25 years showed significantly more positive personality.

SECTION - IV

CORRELATIONAL ANALYSES

This section includes the results regarding the relationships between the personality and hostel environment adjustment variables. This section was sub-categorised in to three parts. First-part included with the Inter correlation matrix of personality dimensions. Second part consists of the inter-correlation matrix of hostel adjustment dimensions and the third part consists of the inter correlation matrix between the personality adjustment variables with hostel adjustment variables.

1. Inter Correlation of Personality Adjustment

The inter correlations between the variables of personality adjustment are presented in Table 4. 23.

Table 4.23
Intercorrelation Matrix of Personality Dimensions
(N=556)

Dimensions	*Loneliness*	*Emotionality*	*Health adjustment*	*Academic adjustment*	*Social adjustment*
Self pity	0.38**	0.55**	0.55**	0.49**	0.54**
Loneliness		0.43**	0.32**	0.25**	0.33**
Emotionality			0.46**	0.43**	0.53**
Health Adjustment				0.36**	0.45**
Academic Adjustment					0.46**

** $P < 0.01$.

It can be noted that all the independent variables are significantly and positively related between them. These correlations indicate that the degree of personality adjustment increases between them.

The self-pity dimension is relationship with other dimensions like loneliness, emotionality, health adjustment, academic adjustment and social adjustments are statistically significant and positively correlated. The self-pity dimension measuring the maladjustment caused by self inferior feelings like disappointments, feeling of sadness, inferiority complex, self tortures etc. The results indicate that when the self-pity increased, the maladjustment related to other dimensions was increased.

With regard to loneliness the table indicates that it is positively and significantly related to emotionality, health adjustment, academic adjustment and social adjustment dimensions. The loneliness feelings create maladjustment. Due to increase of this maladjustment the related dimensions are also increase to create maladjustments in their dimensions.

The relationship between emotionality and health adjustment, academic adjustment and social adjustments are significant and positive. High emotional feelings create maladjusted managed personality in health, academic and social aspects.

The health adjustment dimension positively and significantly related to academic and social adjustments where as academic adjustment related positively and significantly with social adjustments. If the health adjustments are not good in the hostel students, the maladjustment formed in academic and social adjustments. The degree of maladjustment of academic, cause maladjustment in social adjustments also. The results indicated that the better adjustment in personality adjustment factors leads to better personality adjustment of hostel students.

2. Intercorrelation of Hostel Environment Variables

The intercorrelations of the hostel adjustment dimensions are tabulated in Table 4.24. (*See Table on next page*)

Most of the relationships between the variables are positive and significant.

The room dimension related with toilet, food and dining hall, hostelmates and servants, health and recreation, guest, information, crisis and financial adjustments are significant and positive. When the students maintain the room adjustment properly by maintaining the furniture and maintaining the relationships with roommates, they would have adjusted with the other dimensions also.

The toilet dimension related with hostelmates and servants, health and recreation, information, crisis and financial adjustments are significant and positive. The toilet adjustment related to the bathrooms, cleanliness etc. If the students are better adjusted in this dimension the related dimensions are also measures the positive adjustments.

With regard to food and dining hall dimension related positively and significantly with other dimensions like hostelmates and servants, crisis, financial and spiritual adjustments. When the students are satisfied in food the related dimensions are also adjusted.

The hostelmates and servants dimension positively and significantly related with health and recreation, guest, information, crisis, financial and spiritual adjustments. If the students maintain cordial relationships with others hostelmates and make the servants to work, such type of positive aspects of adjustments related to positive adjustments with other dimensions.

Table 4.24

Intercorrelation Matrix of Hostel Environment Dimensions

(N=556)

Dimensions	*Toilet*	*Food & Dining Hall*	*Hostelmates & Servants*	*Health & Recreation*	*Guest*	*Information*	*Crisis*	*Financial*	*Spiritual*
Room	0.16**	0.12**	0.22**	0.28**	0.13**	0.23**	0.19**	0.35**	0.01
Toilet		0.04	0.11**	0.09*	0.03	0.11**	0.10**	0.12**	0.04
Food & Dining Hall			0.16**	0.02	0.00	-0.01	0.16**	0.17**	0.15**
Hostelmates & Servants				0.17**	0.15**	0.11**	0.29**	0.18**	0.34**
Health & Recreation					0.13**	0.31**	0.23**	0.27**	0.02
Guest						0.18**	0.18**	0.08	0.13**
Information							0.26**	0.21**	0.08
Crisis								0.14**	0.30**
Financial									0.02

* P < 0. 05.

** P < 0. 01.

Related to health and recreation dimension, the relationship with other dimensions like guest, information, crisis and financial adjustments are positive and significant. Maintain good health habits, exercises etc. are the positive adjustment aspects. The other dimensions are also positively adjusted in their relationship with health and recreation.

The guest dimension significantly and positively related with information, crisis and spiritual adjustments. If the hostel students have a good adjustment towards guests, they would have adjusted better in those significant dimensions also.

The information dimension significant and positively related with crisis and financial adjustments. When the hostel students better adjusted better in information, they have better adjustments in those two aspects also. The crisis dimension in relationship with financial and spiritual adjustments significant and positive. When the students adjusted better in crisis adjustment, they would have adjusted better in those two dimensions also. The results indicated that the better adjustment in hostel adjustment factors leads to better hostel adjustment in hostel students.

3. Intercorrelation of Personality and Hostel Adjustment

The intercorrelation matrix of personality and hostel adjustment variables is tabulated in Table 4.25. (*See on next page*)

Most of the values in the table are significant.

The discussions of the not significant values are neglected; only the significant values are discussed. All the significant values are neglected, only the significant values negatively correlated because the personality adjustment variables measure the degree of maladjustment, whereas the hostel adjustment variables measure the degree of adjustment.

Table 4.25
Intercorrelation Matrix of Personality and Hostel Environment Adjustment Variables
(N=556)

Dimensions	*Room*	*Toilet*	*Food & Dining Hall*	*Hostel-mates and Servants*	*Health and Recreation*	*Guest*	*Information*	*Crisis*	*Financial*	*Spiritual*
Self pity	-0.18**	-0.10**	-0.15**	-0.16**	-0.21**	-0.08	-0.07	-0.16**	-0.20**	-0.18**
Loneliness	-0.12**	-0.02	-0.15**	-0.15**	-0.14**	0.01	-0.15**	-0.13**	-0.14**	-0.14**
Emotionality	-0.24**	-0.10**	-0.15**	-0.16**	-0.19**	-0.11**	-0.12**	-0.16**	-0.13**	-0.08
Health Adjustment	-0.13**	-0.16**	-0.17**	-0.15**	-0.08	-0.11**	-0.01	-0.12**	-0.20**	-0.13**
Academic Adjustment	-0.12**	-0.06	-0.07	-0.10**	-0.14**	-0.14**	-0.01	-0.11**	-0.12**	-0.16**
Social Adjustment	-0.25**	-0.15**	-0.15**	-0.17**	-0.22**	-0.06	-0.06	-0.10**	-0.20**	-0.09*

* $P < 0.05$.

** $P < 0.01$.

The table shows that the self-pity dimension related to room toilet, food and dining hall, hostelmates and servants, health and recreation, crisis, financial and spiritual adjustments are significant and negatively correlated. The self-pity dimension measuring the disappointments, inferior feelings, sadness etc, of the students. The hostel students with self-pity not maintain the room in an orderly way. It was not possible to maintain clean habits of toilet adjustment. Students cannot take food with satisfaction. They would have not interested to maintain relationships with others. They cannot look after their health. It was not possible to overcome from crisis. It was not possible to spend and not possible for spirituality. So the related dimensions are negatively correlated.

The loneliness dimension related with room, food and dining hall, hostelmates and servants, health and recreation, information, crisis, financial and spiritual adjustments are significant and negative. When the loneliness dimension was low in students, there was a chance of better adjustments towards the environmental factors. When the students are maladjusted, the environmental factors adjustments would be reduced.

The emotionality dimension related with room, toilet, food and dining hall, hostelmates and servants, health and recreation, guest, information, crisis and financial adjustments are significant and negative. When the students are emotionally maladjusted, they have maladjusted in the hostel adjustment factors also. When the students with high emotionality, showed the anxiety or anger on other hostel factors.

Related to health adjustment dimension in relationship with other factors like room, toilet, food and dining hall, hostelmates and servants, guest, crisis, financial and spiritual adjustments are significant and negative. If the health habits of the hostel students are good, then there is a possibility of better adjustment towards the situational factors of the hostel.

The relationship with academic adjustment with other factors like room, hostelmates and servants, health and recreation, guest, crisis, financial and spiritual adjustments are significant and negative. When the students are adjusted better in academic aspects, certainly they would have adjusted on the situational factors of the hostel.

The social adjustment dimension in relationship with room, toilet, food and dining hall, hostelmates and servants, health and recreation, crisis, financial and spiritual adjustments are significant and negative. If the social relationships of hostel students are better, then the other factors are also adjusted better. Overall the results indicated that the better personality adjustment leads to better hostel adjustment in hostel students.

Summary of the Findings Regarding Correlation Analysis

The personality and hostel adjustment dimensions were measuring the respective quality. Verbally they are different whereas in social situations, the dimensions collectively measure the adjustments. It means, there is an overlapping of other dimensions done for measuring a single dimension. Personality adjustment is a collective behaviour so that the dimensions collectively measure the personality adjustment. The psychological, sociological, environmental factors intermingled with the life situations in a hostel. So the distinguished variations were collectively measured in hostel.

It is not possible to study the whole personality adjustment of hostel students in all the dimensions of adjustments related to psychological, sociological and environmental factors. Only the comparisons related to personality and hostel adjustment dimensions were possible to measure and study.

Hence, the present study focused on comparisons of the personality and hostel adjustment factors across the individual factor in an organised and systematic way. The statistically significant values and their discussion were noted and from the results certain conclusions are presented in the next chapter.

The objective of the correlation analysis is to examine the relationship between personality and hostel environmental adjustment dimensions. The hypothesis constructed for this, is the positive personality factors leads to better hostel environmental adjustment.

The findings revealed that healthy personality factors leads to better hostel environment adjustment. The above-mentioned hypothesis is consistent with the findings. Therefore, the hypothesis is validated and accepted.

5

FINDINGS, CONCLUSIONS, RECOMMENDATIONS AND SUGGESTIONS

The present study is conducted to examine the personality and adjustment to hostel environment among university students. A review of literature on select variables has been carried out and it has been observed the personality and environmental factors on student adjustments. Some hostel studies are also kept under the related studies.

Overall the hostel studies indicated that the personality as well as environmental factors influence the adjustment of the students. Most of the studies concluded that the better personality and environmental factors leads to better adjustments of the students.

The major objectives of this study are: To examine the personality of hostel students and the impact of individual factors on their personality; To examine the adjustment to hostel environment by students and the impact of individual factors on hostel environmental adjustment; and To examine the relationships between personality and hostel environmental adjustment dimensions.

On the basis of the above objectives, the researcher selected two Indian adjustment inventories, which were constructed and standardised for Indian settings: 1. Personality Adjustment Inventory was constructed and standardised by C.P. Sharma, (1972), it consists of 54 items with six dimensions. The six personality adjustment dimensions are self-pity, loneliness, emotionality, health adjustment, academic adjustment and social adjustment; 2. Hostel Adjustment Inventory was constructed and standardised by Krishnan and Sundaram (1992). It consists of 40 items with ten dimensions. The ten dimensions of hostel adjustment are room, toilet, food and dining hall, hostelmates and servants, health and recreation, guest, information, crisis, financial and spiritual adjustments.

Apart from these personality and hostel adjustment dimensions, some individual variables included in the study are age, sex, nationality, faculty, permanent place of residence, previous and present hostel experiences and economic status of the hostel students. The internal consistency reliabilities and validity of the scales have been found to be acceptable.

The final study was conducted on a sample of 556 hostel students of Andhra University, Visakhapatnam. The samples of respondents have been categorised according to the individual factors. The data was analysed by using 't' tests, One-way analysis of variance and multivariate analysis tests and Pearson's product moment coefficient of correlations.

FINDINGS OF THE STUDY

The major findings of the study are the following:

1. Personality

1. The hostel students of 25 years of age and above are adjusted better than below 25 years of age in emotionality dimension.
2. The male hostel students are adjusted better than female hostel students in loneliness and emotionality dimensions whereas female students adjusted better than male students in academic adjustment dimension.

3. Foreign students are adjusted better than Indian students in emotionality and academic adjustment dimensions.

4. Urban hostel students are adjusted better than rural hostel students in academic adjustment dimension.

5. The previous hostel experience of the students has no influence on the dimensions of personality adjustment.

6. Medical hostel students are adjusted better than arts, science, engineering and law students in self-pity dimension. Law students are adjusted better than arts, science and engineering students in self-pity dimension. Engineering students are adjusted better than arts and science students in self-pity dimension. Science students are adjusted better than arts students in self-pity dimension.

7. Students with more than four years hostel experience are better adjusted than less experienced in self pity and health adjustment.

8. The economically rich students adjusted better than the poor and middle class students in self-pity dimension. The middle class I students are adjusted better than poor, middle class II, III and rich status students in loneliness dimension. The middle class III group students are adjusted better than poor, middle class I, II and rich hostel students in emotionality. The middle class III students are adjusted better than poor, middle class I, II and rich status students in health adjustment dimension. The rich groups of hostel students are adjusted better than poor and middle class groups' students in academic adjustment dimension. The middle class III group students are adjusted better than poor, middle class I, II and rich students in social adjustment dimension.

2. Hostel Adjustment

1. The hostel students' age group of 25 years and above adjusted better than the age below 25 years students in crisis dimension.

2. Female hostel students are adjusted better than male hostel students in room, toilet, and financial adjustment dimensions. Male students are adjusted better than female students in health and recreation and crisis dimensions.

3. Indian students are adjusted better than foreign students in room, hostelmates and servants, and financial adjustment dimensions. Foreign students are adjusted better than Indian students in guest and spiritual adjustment dimensions.

4. Urban hostel students are better adjusted than rural hostel students in crisis and spiritual adjustment dimensions.

5. Inexperienced hostel students adjusted better than previous experienced hostel students in food and dining hall and financial adjustment dimensions.

6. Medical students are adjusted better than arts, science, engineering and law students in room adjustment. Engineering students are adjusted better than arts, science and law students in room adjustment. Law students are adjusted better than arts and science students in room adjustment. Arts students are adjusted better than science students in room adjustment.

7. 4 years present hostel experienced students are adjusted better than one year, 2 years, 3 years and five years students in toilet adjustment. 5 years present hostel experienced students are adjusted better than one year, 2 years, 3 years and 4 years students in crisis adjustment. 4 years present experienced hostel students are adjusted better than one year, 2 years, 3 years and five year's students in spiritual adjustment.

8. The middle class III group students adjusted better than poor, middle class I, II, and rich students in room adjustment. The middle class III group students adjusted better than poor, middle class I, II and rich students in toilet adjustment. The middle class III group students adjusted better than poor, middle class I, II and rich group

students in food and dining hall adjustment. The rich groups of students are adjusted better than poor and middle class groups in guest adjustment. The middle class III group of students adjusted better than poor, middle class I, II and rich group of students in crisis adjustment. The middle class II group of students adjusted better than poor, middle class I, III and rich group of students in financial adjustment. The rich group of students adjusted better than poor and middle class groups' students in spiritual adjustment. The intercorrelations between the personality adjustment dimensions with the hostel adjustment dimensions are negatively correlated for the most of the dimensions. This indicates that better personality adjustment leads to better hostel adjustment.

All the results and findings presented above are generalised in the present study. Firstly the personality adjustment dimensions generalised in the comparisons across different individual factors of the hostel students. Secondly, the hostel adjustment dimensions generalised in comparison across different individual factors of the hostel students. Finally, the relationship between the variables related to personality and hostel adjustments are generalised.

CONCLUSIONS OF THE STUDY

1. Age of the hostel students in the aspects of adjustment is an important factor. The age groups of 25 years and above hostel students are adjusted better in personality adjustment and hostel adjustment factors like emotionality and crisis.

2. Concerned to the aspect of sex, female students are better in academic adjustment and better in hostel adjustment factors, but suffered with loneliness and emotionality. Whereas male students are strong in loneliness and emotionality dimensions.

3. In the variable of nationality, foreign students are better emotional and academic adjustment in personality adjustment factors and better adjustment in guest and spiritual adjustments related to hostel adjustment factors.

4. Indian students are adjusted better in room adjustment, hostelmates and servants' adjustment and financial adjustment related to hostel adjustment factors.

5. Related to the permanent place of residence, the urban students are better in personality as well as hostel adjustment factors.

6. In the faculty studies medical students are better adjusted in both personality and hostel adjustment factors. Over all professional students are better adjusted than non-professional students.

7. The previous hostel experience of the hostel students does not influence the personality adjustment whereas, the students having no earlier experience in hostel life adjusted better in some hostel adjustment factors like food and dining hall and financial adjustments.

8. In the present hostel experience of hostel students, the senior students of 3rd, 4th year students got better personality adjustments in self pity and health adjustment, whereas in hostel adjustment factors, better adjustment in toilet, hostelmates and servants, crisis and spiritual adjustments.

9. In the economic status of hostel students, the middle class III and rich status students got better personality adjustment in self pity, emotionality, health adjustment, academic adjustment and social adjustments whereas the middle class groups got better loneliness adjustments than poor and rich students. In hostel adjustment factors also the middle class II, III and rich status students got better adjustments in room, toilet, food and dining hall, guest, crisis, financial and spiritual adjustments.

10. The relationship between personality adjustment factors and hostel adjustment factors are positive and they are measuring the better adjustments.

The relationship between the factors of personality adjustment with hostel adjustment is negative since the personality adjustments measuring the degree of maladjustment of hostel students. Overall view the better personality adjustment leads to better hostel adjustment of the hostel students. The better personality adjustment of hostel students leads to better academic, emotional and social adjustments.

RECOMMENDATIONS OF THE STUDY

1. The age groups of below 25 years hostel students are emotionally high. The students, who are suffering with not only emotional problems, any psychological problems are recommended to take psychological help from the psychological counselling cell.
2. Concerned to female hostel students, they are suffered with loneliness and emotionality. The girl students who are suffering with psychological problems are also recommended to take psychological help from the psychological counselling cell.
3. Related to the health adjustment and emotional adjustment of female students 'slim gym' could be established in ladies hostels for physical exercises and for the relaxation techniques, yoga training is recommended.
4. The hostel students may be provided with a more conductive atmosphere to live and financial aid for the needy to bring out the best from them, especially for the hostel students of low economic status.
5. The student resident hall for the foreign students within the campus for both male and female foreign students is recommended, so that their adjustments are better than Indian students.
6. Rural background students need English language skills training and also vocational counselling for their better placements after completion of their respective courses.
7. The vocational counselling is also recommended especially for arts students to choose better placements after their completion of courses since their personality and hostel adjustments are low comparatively in all faculties.

SUGGESTIONS FOR FUTURE RESEARCH

1. It may be worth while to include a few personality adjustment variables like locus of control, frustration tolerance, level of aspiration, ego strength, self sufficiency, leadership, neuroticism and psychotism, values, approval-seeking motive, student activism, psychological separation and individuation, perceptions of friends and parents, extraversion, personal authority, etc.
2. It may be useful to include a few hostel adjustment variables like prayer hall, gym, sports and games room, social service like clean and green, rules of discipline and punishment, T.V. and newspaper room, laundry, cultural programmes and functions, etc.
3. It may be worthwhile to include a few individual factors like medium of instruction, socio-economic status, caste, religion, familial background factors, parent child relationships, cross cultural variations, alcohol and drug use, etc.
4. The comparisons across different university hostel students within the state, the comparisons across different university hostel students in the country and the comparisons across different university hostel students in different nations can be done to examine the differences in personality adjustment of hostel students.

BIBLIOGRAPHY

Abe, J., Talbot, D.M., & Geelhoed, R.J. (1998). Effects of a Peer Programme on International Student Adjustment. *Journal of College Student Development, 36(9)*, 539-547.

Adan, A.M., & Felner, R.D. (1995). Ecological Congruence and Adaptation of Minority Youth During the Transition to College. *Journal of Community Psychology*, 23(3), 256-269.

Adler, A. (1930). *The Science of Living*. New York: Allen and Unwin.

Aggarwal, J.C. (1985). *Educational, Vocational Guidance and Counselling*. Delhi: Doaba House.

Alexander, E.J., & Packiam, S. (1998). The Adjustment Problems of Rural and Urban School going Adolescents. *The Progress of Education, 5*, 107-110.

Allport, G.W. (1961). *Pattern and Growth in Personality*, New York: Holt, Rinehart and Winston.

Aspinwall, L.G., & Taylor, S.E. (1992). Modelling Cognitive Adaptation: A Longitudinal Investigation of the Impact of Individual Differences and Coping on College Adjustment and Performance. *Journal of Personality and Social Psychology*, 63(6), 989-1003.

Bajpai, S. (1999). Effects of Caste Belongingness on Adjustment of High School Girls. *The Progress of Education*, 12, 274-277.

Barratt, M.F., & Huba, M.E. (1994). Factors Related to International Undergraduate Student Adjustment in an American Community. *College Student Journal*, 28(4), 422-436.

Barthelemy, K.J., & Fine, M. A. (1995). The Relations Between Residence Hall Climate and Adjustment in College Students. *College Student Journal*, 29(4), 465-475.

Bell, H.M. (1962). *Manuel, Bell Adjustment Inventory* (Revised Student form, p. 3). California.

Bernard, L.C., Hutchison, S., Lavin, A., & Pennington, P. (1996). Ego-strength, Hardiness, Self-esteem, Self-efficacy, Optimism and Maladjustment: Health-related Personality Constructs and the "Big Five" Model of Personality. *Assessment*, 3(2), 115-131.

Berndt, T.J., Miller, K.E., & Park, K. (1989). Adolescents' Perceptions of Friends' and Parents' Influence on Aspects of Their School Adjustment. *Journal of Early Adolescence*, 9(4), 419-435.

Bettencourt, B.A., Chartton, K., Eubanks, J., & Kernahan, C. (1999). Development of Collective Self-esteem Among Students: Predicting Adjustment to College. *Basis & Applied Social Psychology*, 21(3), 213-222.

Bhatia, H.R. (1965). *Elements of Social Psychology*. Bombay, India: Manaktalas.

Bhatnagar, R.P. (1968). A Study of Some of the Personality Factors as Predictors of Academic Achievement. *C.I.E. Studies in Education and Psychology*, (P.63). New Delhi: National Council of Educational Research and Training.

Boring (1948). *Foundations of Psychology*, New York: John Wiley & Sons Inc.

Bridges, K.R. (1991, June). Psychology of Adjustment at Research Universities. *Psychological Reports*, 68(pt2), 1130.

Brooks, J.H., & DuBois, D. L. (1995). Individual and Environmental Predictors of Adjustment During the First Year of College. *Journal of the College Student Development*, 36(4), 347-360.

Buch, M.B. (Ed.) (1991). *Survey of Research in Education*, New Delhi: NCERT.

Carlisle-Frank, P.L. (1992). The Relocation Experience: Analysis of Factors Thought to Influence Adjustment to Transition. *Psychological Reports*, 70(3, pt 1), 835-838.

Cattell, R.B. (1950). *Personality, A Systematic Theoretical and Factual Study*. New York: McGraw Hill Book Company, Inc.

Chartrand, J.M. (1990). A Causal Analysis to Predict the Personal and Academic Adjustment of Non-traditional Students. *Journal of Counselling Psychology*, 37(1), 65-73.

Chartrand, J. M. (1992). An Empirical Test of a Model of Non-traditional Student Adjustment. *Journal of Counselling Psychology*, 39(2), 193-202.

Chaudhary, B.K., & Sinha, R. B. (1992). A Study of Adjustment in Relation to Some Personality Factors. *Indian Journal of Psychometry* and *Education*, 23(1), 33-36b.

Chaudhury, P.R., & Basu, J. (1998). Parent-child Relationship School Achievement and Adjustment of Adolescent Boys. *Journal of Community Guidance and Research*, 15(2), 215-266.

Chauhan, S.S. (1979). *Advanced Educational Psychology*, New Delhi: Vikas Publishing House Pvt. Ltd.

Cherian, V.I., & Cherian. L. (1998). University Students' Adjustment Problems. *Psychological Reports*, 82(3 pt 2), 1135-1138.

Chiu, M.L. (1995). The Influence of Anticipatory Fear on Foreign Student Adjustment: An Exploratory Study. *International Journal of Intercultural Relations*, 19(1), 1-44.

Clinton, A.M., & Anderson, L.R. (1999). Social and Emotional Loneliness: Gender Differences and Relationships with Self-monitoring and Perceived Control. *Journal of Black Psychology*, 25(1), 61-77.

Coe, W.C. (1972). *Challenges of Personal Adjustment*. San Francisco: Rinehart Press.

Coleman, J.C. (1969). *Abnormal Psychology and Modern Life* (3rd Ed.). Bombay, India: Taraporevala, D.B. and Co., (P). Ltd.

Damji, T., Clement, R., & Noels, K.A. (1996). Acculturation Mode, Identity Variation and Psychosocial Adjustment. *Journal of Social Psychology,* 136(4), 493-500.

Dandekar, W.N. (1981). *Psychological Foundations of Education,* Madras, India: McMillan India Limited.

Defour, D.C., & Hirsch, B.J. (1990). The Adaptation of Black Graduate Students: A Social Network Approach. *American Journal of Community Psychology,* 18(3), 487-503.

Dosajh, N.L. (1982). *Advanced Educational Psychology.* New Delhi: Allied Publishers Private Limited.

Essau, C.A., & Trommsdorff, G. (1996). Coping with University - related Problems: A Cross Cultural Comparison. *Journal of Cross-Cultural Psychology, 27(3),* 315-328.

Eysenck, H.J. (1978). *The Structure of Human Personality.* London: Methuen and Co., Ltd.

Eysenck, H.J., & Eysenck, S.B.G. (1975). *Manual of the Eysenck Personality Inventory.* San Diego: Educational and Industrial Testing Services.

Floyd, N.E. (1988). Family Experience and College Residential Adjustment: Case Examples from An Experimental Living-learning Programme. *College Student Journal,* 22(4), 342-348.

Furukawa, T. (1997). Cultural Distance and Its Relationship to Psychological Adjustment of International Exchange Students. *Psychiatry and Clinical. Neuroscience,* 51(3), 87-91.

Furukawa, T., & Shibayama, T. (1993). Predicting Maladjustment of Exchange Students in Different Cultures: A Prospective Study. *Social Psychiatry and Psychiatrical Epidemiology,* 28(3), 142-146.

Garbarino, C., & Strange, C. (1993). College Adjustment and Family Environments of Students Reporting Parental Alcohol Problems. *Journal of College Student Development,* 34(4), 261-266.

Gates, A.S., & Jersild, A.T. (1973). *Educational Psychology,* (p: 614-615), New York: McMillan and Co.

Gerdes, H., & Mallinckrodt, B. (1994). Emotional, Social and Academic Adjustment of College Students: A Longitudinal Study of Retention. *Journal of Counseling and Development*, 72(3), 281-288.

Getzels, J.W., (1975). "A Social Psychology of Education", in Lindzey, G., & Aronson, E (Ed), *The Handbook of Social Psychology*, (2nd Edition, Vol. V). New Delhi: Amerind Publishing Company Pvt., Ltd.

Good, C.V. (1945). *Dictionary of Education*, (p: 6). New York: McGraw Hill Book Co., Inc.

Gorlow, K. (1968). *Readings in the Psychology of Adjustment*. New York: Mc Graw-Hill Book Company.

Grant, L.S., Smith, T. A., Sinclair, J. J., & Salts, C. J. (1993). The Impact of Parental Divorce on College Adjustment. *Journal of Divorce and Remarriage*, 19(1-2), 183-193.

Graziano, W.G., Jensen - Campbell, L.A., & Finch. J.F. (1997). The Self as a Mediator Between Personality and Adjustment. *Journal of Personality and Social Psychology*, 73(2), 392-404.

Greenier, K.D., Kernis, M.H., McNamara, C.W., & Waschull, S.B. (1999). Individual Differences in Reactivity to Daily Events: Examining the Roles of Stability and Level of Self-esteem. *Journal of Personality*, 67(1), 185-208.

Haemmerlie, F.M., Steen, S.C., & Benedicto. J.A. (1994). Undergraduates' Conflictual Independence, Adjustment and Alcohol Use: The Importance of the Mother-student Relationship. *Journal of Clinical Psychology*, 50(4), 644-650.

Halamandaris, K.F., & Power, K.G. (1997). Individual Differences, Dysfunctional Attitudes and Social Support: A Study of the Psycho-social Adjustment to University Life of Home Students. *Personality and Individual Differences*, 1(22), 93-104.

Hall, C.S., & Lindzey, G. (1978). *Theories of Personality* (3rd Ed.). New York: John Wiley & Sons.

Henning, K., Ey, S., & Shaw, D. (1998). Perfectionism, the Imposter Phenomenon and Psychological Adjustment in Medical, Dental, Nursing and Pharmacy Students. *Medical Education*, 32(5), 456-464.

Holmbeck, G.N., & Wandrei, M. L. (1993). Individual and Relational Predictors of Adjustment in First-year College Students. *Journal of Counselling Psychology,* 40(1), 73-78.

Hussain, S., & Kumari, M. (1995). Eysenck's Personality Dimensions in Relation to Ego-strength and Adjustment. *Journal of Personality and Clinical Studies,* 11 (1-2), 43-48.

Ichiyama, M.A., Colbert, D., Laramore, H., & Heim, M. (1993). Self-concealment and Correlates of Adjustment in College Students. *Journal of College Student Psychotherapy,* 7(4), 55-68.

Iwata, O. (1994). The Relationships of Intolerance for Waiting-stress with Health and Personality, 25th International Congress of Psychology (1992, Brussels, Belgium). *Psycho logia: An International Journal of Psychology in the Orient,* 37(2), 81-88.

Jay, G.M., & D' Augelli, A.R. (1991). Social Support and Adjustment to University Life: A Comparison of African-American and White Freshmen. *Journal of Community Psychology,* 19(2), 95-108.

Jayaswal, S. (1974). *Foundations of Educational Psychology.* New Delhi: Arnold Heinemann Publishers (India) Pvt. Ltd.

Jou, Y.H., & Fukada, H. (1995). Effect of Social Support from Various Sources on the Adjustment of Chinese Students in Japan. *Journal of Social Psychology,* 135(3), 305-311.

Jou, Y.H., & Fukada, H. (1996a). Cross-cultural Adjustment of Chinese Students in Japan. *Psychological Reports,* 78(2), 435-444.

Jou, Y.H., & Fukada, H. (1996b). Influence of Social Supports and Personality on Adjustment of Chinese Students in Japan. *Journal of Applied Social Psychology,* 26(20), 1795-1802.

Kaczmarek, P.G., Matlock, G, Merta, R, & Ames, M.H. (1994). An Assessment of International College Student's Adjustment. *International Journal for the Advancement of Counselling,* 17(4), 241-247.

Kakkar, S.B. (1993). *Educational Psychology.* New Delhi: Prentice-Hall of India Pvt. Ltd.

Kasinath, H.M. (1991). Adjustment Between Migrated Hindi and Non-Hindi Speaking Students Studying in Jawahar Navodaya Vidyalayas. *The Progress of Education*, 9, 8-10.

Kasinath, M.M. (1990). Adjustment in Navodaya Vidyalayas. *The Progress of Education*, 1, 8-11.

Kenny, M.E., & Donaldson, G.A. (1992). The Relationship of Parental Attachment of First Year College Women. *Journal of College Student Development*, 33 (5), 431-438.

Kenny, M.E., & Rice. K.G., (1995). Attachment to Parents and Adjustment in Late Adolescent College Students: Current Status, Applications, and Future Considerations. Counselling Psychologist, 23(3), 433-456.

Kenrick, D.T., McCreath, H.E., Govern, J., & King, R. (1990). Person Environment Intersections: Everyday Settings and Common Trait Dimensions. *Journal of Personality and Social Psychology*, 58(4), 685-698.

Khan, R. (1991). Study of Adjustment in Relation to Some Personality and Personal Background Factors Among College Students. *Indian Psychological Review*, 36(1-2), 38-39.

Krishnan, K., & Sundaram. A.M. (1992). Hostel Adjustment Inventory. *The Educational Review*, 11, 181-185.

Kulshrestha, S.P. (1979). *Educational Psychology*. Meerut, India: Loyal Book Depot.

Kundu, C.L., & Tutoo, D.N. (1976). *Educational Psychology*. New Delhi: Sterling Publishers Pvt. Ltd.

Lakshmi, V. (1998). Adjustment of Androgynous Persons. *Praachi Journal of Psycho-cultural Dimensions*, 14(2), 149-152.

Lapsley, D.K., Rice, K.G., & Fitz Gerald, D.P. (1990). Adolescent Attachment Identity and Adjustment to College: Implications for the Continuity of Adaptation Hypothesis. *Journal of Counselling and Development*, 68(5), 561-565.

Lapsley, D.K., Rice, K.G., & Shadid, G.E. (1989). Psychological Separation and Adjustment to College. *Journal of Counselling Psychology*, 36(3), 286-294.

Lazarus, R.S. (1976). *Patterns of Adjustment*. Tokyo, Japan: McGraw-Hill, Kogakusha Pvt. Ltd.

Lecci, L., Okun, M. A., & Karoly, P. (1994). Life Regrets and Current Goals as Predictors of Psychological Adjustment. *Journal of Personality and Social Psychology*, 66(4), 731-741.

Leong, F.T.L., Bonz, M.H., & Zachar, P. (1997). Coping Styles as Predictors of College Adjustment Among Freshmen. *Counselling Psychology Quarterly*, 10(2), 211-220.

Leong, F.T., Mallinckrodt, B., & Kralj, M.M. (1990). Cross-cultural Variations in Stress and Adjustment Among Asian and Caucasian Graduate Students. *Journal of Multicultural Counselling and Development*, *18(1)*, 19-28.

Lindgren, H.C. (1959). *Psychology of Personal and Social Adjustment* (2nd Ed). New York: American Book Company.

Lopez, F.G. (1991). Patterns of Family Conflict and their Relation to College Student Adjustment. *Journal of Counselling and Development*, 69(3), 257-260.

Mangal, S.K. (1989). *Abnormal Psychology*. New Delhi: Sterling Publishers Pvt. Ltd.

Martin, N.K., & Dixon, P.N. (1989). The Effects of Freshman Orientation and Locus of Control on Adjustment to College. *Journal of College Student Development*, 30(4), 362-367.

Martin, N.K., & Dixon, P.N. (1994). The Effects of Freshman Orientation and Locus of Control on Adjustment to College: A Follow-up Study. *Social Behaviour and Personality*, 22(2), 201-208.

Mishra, S., & Singh, R.D. (1998). Personality Adjustment of Graduates with Reference to Their Socio-economic Status. *Praachi Journal of Psycho-cultural Dimensions*, 14(1), 43-44.

Mitra, S.K. & Bhatkal, R.G., Eds. (1972). *A Survey of Research in Psychology*: A Project Sponsored by the Indian Council of Social Science Research, New Delhi. Bombay, India: Popular Prakashan.

Miya, I., & Krishna, K.P. (1996). Adjustment Problem Among Socio-economically Deprived Adolescents. *Indian Journal of Psychological Issues*, 4(1), 32-35.

Mohan, J., & Kaur, M. (1991). A Study of Adjustment of University Research Scholars in Relation to Their Values and Socio-economic Status. *Indian Psychological Review*, 36(5-6), 9-18.

Monroe, P. (Ed.) (1990). *International Encyclopaedia of Education*. New Delhi: Cosmo Publications.

Montgomery, R.L., & Haemmerlie, F.M. (1993). Undergraduate Adjustment to College, Drinking Behaviour and Fraternity Membership. *Psychological Reports*, 73(3, pt 1), 801-802.

Mooney, S.P., Sherman, M.F., & Lopresto, C.T. (1991). Academic Locus of Control Self-esteem and Perceived Distance from Home as Predictors of College Adjustment. *Journal of Counselling and Development*. 69(5), 445-448.

Mukhopadyay, P., De. S., Chattopadhyay. K., & Biswas, D. (1996). "Deprivation": Its Impact on Arousal Modulation and Adjustment. A Psycho-physiological Approach. *Indian Journal of Clinical Psychology*, 23(2), 161-169.

Nelson, W.L., Hughes, H.M., Handal, P., & Katz, B. (1993). The Relationship of Family Structure and Family Conflict to Adjustment in Young Adult College Students. *Adolescence*, 28(109), 29-40.

Odera, P., & Hasan, Q. (1995). Problems of Adjustment to a Foreign Culture. *Journal of Community Guidance and Research*, 12(1), 63-75.

O'Connell, V., & O'Connell, A. (1974). *Choice and Change: An Introduction to Psychology of Growth*. New Jersey: Prentice–Hall, Inc. Englewood Cliffs.

Pennebaker, J.W., Colder, M., & Sharp, L.K. (1990). Accelerating the Coping Process. *Journal of Personality and Social Psychology*, 58(3), 528-537.

Ponraj, J.P., & Packiam, S. (1993). Adjustment Problems of Adolescents. *The Progress of Education*, 2, 42-45.

Prasad, R.S. (1993). A Study of Adjustment in Relation to Social Integration and Achievement of the Students of Residential Schools, Waltair. *Unpublished Ph.D. Thesis*, Andhra University, Visakhapatnam: India.

Protinsky, H., & Gilkey, J.K. (1996). An Empirical Investigation of the Construct of Personality Authority in Late Adolescent Women and Their Level of College Adjustment. *Adolescence,* 31(122), 291-295.

Rajan, S.S., Ashrafullah, A.M., & Rajan, V.N. (1988). Adjustment Problems of Professional and Non-professional College Students. *The Progress of Education,* 3, 56-59.

Ramanaiah, N.V., Byravan, A., & ThuHien, N. (1996). Weinberger Adjustment Typology and the Five-factor Model of Personality. *Psychological Reports,* 78(2), 432-434.

Rao, V., & Yadav, S. (1992). Adjustment Problems of Adolescent Girls in Relation to Family Size and Birth Order. *Journal of Community Guidance and Research,* 9(1), 51-57.

Ray, A. (1992). Personality Adjustment and Academic Achievement. *Psychological Research Journal,* 16(2), 43-51.

Reggio, R.E., Watring, K.P., & Throckmorton, B. (1993). Social Skills, Social Support and Psychosocial Adjustment. *Personality and Individual Differences,* 15(3), 275-280.

Rehulkova, O., Blatny, M., & Osecka, L. (1995). Adolescents Coping Styles: A Relation to the Temperament. *Studia Psychologica,* 37(3), 159-161.

Rice, K.G. (1992). Separation-individuation and Adjustment to College: A Longitudinal Study. *Journal of Counselling Psychology,* 39(2), 203-213.

Rice, K.G., Cole, D.A., & Lapsley, D.K. (1990). Separation-individuation, Family Cohesion and Adjustment to College: Measurement Validation and Test of a Theoretical Model. *Journal of Counselling Psychology,* 37(2), 195-202.

Rice, K.G., & Whaley, T.J. (1994). A Short-term Longitudinal Study of within Semester Stability and Change in Attachment and College Student Adjustment. *Journal of College Student Development,* 35(5), 324-330.

Rim, Y. (1989). Self-confrontation and Coping Styles. *Personality and Individual Differences,* 10(9), 1011-1014.

Robbins, S.B., Lese, K.P., & Herrick, S.M. (1993). Interactions Between Goal Instability and Social Support on College Freshman Adjustment. *Journal of Counselling and Development,* 71(3), 343-348.

Ruch, F.L. (1970). *Psychology and Life.* Bombay, India: D.B. Taraporewala Sons and Co.

Sakofske, D.H., & Kelly, I.W. (1995). Coping and Personality. *Psychological Reports,* 77(2), 481-482.

Sanford, N. (1970). *Issues in Personality Theory.* San Francisco: Jossey-Bass Inc. Publishers.

Schultheiss, D.E., Palladine., & Blustein, D.L. (1994). Role of Adolescent-parent Relationships in College Student Development and Adjustment. *Journal of Counselling Psychology,* 41(2), 248-255.

Schwitzer, A.M., McGovern, T.V., & Robbins, S.B. (1991). Adjustment Outcomes of a Freshman Seminar: A Utilisation Focussed Approach. *Journal of College Student Development,* 32(6), 484-489.

Schwitzer, A.M., Robbins, S.B., & McGovern, T.V. (1993). Influences of Goal Instability and Social Support on College Adjustment. *Journal of College Student Development,* 34(1), 21-25.

Shaffer, G. W., & Lazarus, R.S. (1952). *Fundamental Concepts in Clinical Psychology.* New York: McGraw-Hill.

Shaffer, L.F., & Shoben, E.J. (1956). *The Psychology of Adjustment.* Boston: Houghton Mifflin Co.

Shaffer, L.S. (1961). *Foundations of Psychology* (Ed. p: 511). New York: Boring, Longfield and Weld, John Willey and Sons.

Sharma, C.P. (1972). *Manual for Personality Adjustment Inventory.* Agra, India: Agra Psychological Research Cell.

Sharma, K., Verma, B.P., & Kumar, R. (1989). The Relationship of Achievement Motivation, Adjustment and Self-concept with Academic Performance of the Students at +2 stage. *The Progress of Education,* 2, 30-32.

Silverthorn, N.A., & Gekoski, W.L. (1995). Social Desirability Effects on Measures of Adjustment to University, Independence from Parents, and Self-efficacy. *Journal of Clinical Psychology,* 51(2), 244-251.

Singh, R.S. (1992). Student Activism in Relation to Adjustment: A Socio-psychological Study. *Indian Psychological Review,* 38(6-7), 1-5.

Smith, H. C. (1961). Personality Adjustment. New York: McGraw-Hill Book Co.

Smith, M.A., & Baker, R. W. (1987). Freshman Decidedness Regarding Academic Major and Adjustment to College. *Psychological Reports,* 61(3), 847-853.

Sood, R. (1992). Academic Achievement in Relation to Adjustment. *Journal of Psychological Research,* 36(1), 1-4.

Strange, A.A. (1998). Family Context Variables and the Development of Self-regulation in College Students. *Adolescence,* 33(129), 17-31.

Street, S., & Kromrey, J. D. (1994). Differences in Adjustment Issues for Male and Female Adolescents. *Special Services in the Schools,* 8(2), 143-154.

Sujatha., S., Gaonkar, V., Khadi, P., & Katarki, P.A. (1993). Factors Influencing Adjustment Among Adolescents. *Indian Psychological Review,* 40(1-2), 35-40.

Swami, P.M. (1993). The Adjustment of Orphan Students in Comparison with Normal Students. *The Progress of Education,* 6, 125-128.

Takahashi, K., & Majima, N. (1994). Transition from Home to College Dormitory: The Role of Pre-established Affective Relationships in Adjustment to a New Life. *Journal of Research on Adolescence,* 4(3), 367-384.

Tallent, N. (1978). *Psychology of Adjustment: Understanding Ourselves and Others* (p: 2). New York: D.Van Nostrand Company.

Tanaka, T., Takai, J., Kohyama, T., & Fujihara, T. (1994). Adjustment Patterns of International Students in Japan. *International Journal of Intercultural Relations,* 18(1), 55-75.

Terry, D.J. (1994). Determinants of Coping: The Role of Stable and Situational Factors. *Journal of Personality and Social Psychology,* 66(5), 895-910.

Thorpe, L.P., & Schmuller, A.M. (1965). *Personality: An Interdisciplinary Approach*. New Delhi: D.Van Nostrand Company, Inc. New York, Affiliated East-West Press Pvt. Ltd.

Tiwari, S., & Pooranchand, L.J. (1994). A Study of Adjustment Among High and Low Achieving Adolescents. *Asian Journal of Psychological Education, 27(5-6)*, 28-29.

Tloczynski, J. (1994). A Preliminary Study of Opening-up Meditation College Adjustment and Self-actualisation. *Psychological Reports,* 75(1 pt 2), 449-450.

Tobacyk, J.J., & Driggers, E.C. (1989). Self-monitoring as a Moderator of Relationships Between Traditional Religious Belief and Personality Adjustment. *Psychological Reports,* 65(3, pt 2), 1185-1186.

Valentiner, D.P., Holahan, C. J., & Moos, R.H. (1994). Social Supports, Appraisals of Event Controllability and Coping: An Integrative Model. *Journal of Personality and Social Psychology,* 66(6), 1094-1102.

Verma, B.P., & Swain, B.C. (1991). Self-concept of Adolescent Students as a Determinant of Their Personality Adjustment. *The Progress of Education, 1*, 5-9.

Vonhaller, G.B. (1970). *Psychology* (p: 426). New York: Harper International Edition.

Weiss, L.H., & Schwarz, J.C. (1996). The Relationship Between Parenting Types and Older Adolescents' Personality, Academic Achievement, Adjustment and Substance Use. *Child Development,* 67(5), 2101-2114.

Zakahi, W.R., Jordan, F.F., & Christophel, D. (1993). Social Adjustment to College: Communication Apprehension and Social Network Development Among College Students. *Communication Research Reports,* 10(1), 39-46.

References

Bhaskara Rao, Digumarti (1994). *Scientific Aptitude.* New Delhi: Ashish Publishing House. ISBN 81-7024-658-X.

Bhaskara Rao, Digumarti (1995). *Animal Kingdom.* New Delhi: Discovery Publishing House. ISBN 81-7141-274-2.

Bhaskara Rao, Digumarti (1995). *Batracology.* New Delhi: Discovery Publishing House. ISBN 81-7141-279-3.

Bhaskara Rao, Digumarti (1997). *Scientific Attitude.* New Delhi: Discovery Publishing House. ISBN 81-7141-381-1.

Bhaskara Rao, Digumarti (1996). *Scientific Attitude vis-à-vis Scientific Aptitude.* New Delhi: Discovery Publishing House. ISBN 81-7141-308-0.

Bhaskara Rao, Digumarti (2004). *Scientific Attitude, Scientific Aptitude and Achievement.* New Delhi: Discovery Publishing House. ISBN 81-7141-781-7.

Bhaskara Rao, Digumarti (2004). *Educational Administration.* New Delhi: Discovery Publishing House. ISBN 81-7141-842-2.

Bhaskara Rao, Digumarti (2004). *Issues in School Education.* New Delhi: Discovery Publishing House. ISBN 81-8356-025-3.

Bhaskara Rao, Digumarti, Editor (1996). *Encyclopaedia of Education For All,* 5 Volumes. New Delhi: APH Publishing Corporation. ISBN 81-7024-759-4 (set).

Vol. I *Education For All: The World Conference.* ISBN 81-7024-760-8.

Vol. II *Education For All: The EPA-9 Summit.* ISBN 81-7024-761-6.

Vol. III *Education For All: Quality Education For All.* ISBN 81-7024-762-6.

Vol. IV *Education For All: Planning and Monitoring.* ISBN 81-7024-763-4.

Vol. V *Education For All: The Indian Scenario.* ISBN 81-7024-764-0.

Bhaskara Rao, Digumarti, Editor (1996). *National Policy on Education*, 2 Volumes. New Delhi: Anmol Publications Pvt. Ltd. ISBN 81-7488-323-1.

Bhaskara Rao, Digumarti, Editor (1996). *Global Perceptions on Peace Education*, 3 Volumes. New Delhi: Discovery Publishing House. ISBN 81-7141-319-6.

Bhaskara Rao, Digumarti, Editor (1997). *Education for the 21st Century*. New Delhi: Discovery Publishing House. ISBN 81-7141-389-7.

Bhaskara Rao, Digumarti, Editor (1997). *Reflections on Scientific Attitude*. New Delhi: Discovery Publishing House. ISBN 81-7141-319-6.

Bhaskara Rao, Digumarti, Editor (1997). *Success Story of a Primary Education Project*. New Delhi: APH Publishing Corporation. ISBN 81-7024-850-7.

Bhaskara Rao, Digumarti, Editor (1997). *World Food Summit*. New Delhi: Discovery Publishing House. ISBN 81-7141-386-2.

Bhaskara Rao, Digumarti, Editor (1997). *Care the Child*, 2 Volumes. New Delhi: Discovery Publishing House. ISBN 81-7141-394-3.

Bhaskara Rao, Digumarti, Editor (1998). *Earth Summit*, 2 Volumes. New Delhi: Discovery Publishing House. ISBN 81-7141-435-4.

Bhaskara Rao, Digumarti, Editor (1998). *Adolescence Education*. New Delhi: Discovery Publishing House. ISBN 81-7141-432-X.

Bhaskara Rao, Digumarti, Editor (1998). *Community and School Nutrition Education*. New Delhi: Discovery Publishing House. ISBN 81-7141-435-4.

Bhaskara Rao, Digumarti, Editor (1998). *District Primary Education Programme*. New Delhi: Discovery Publishing House. ISBN 81-7141-396-X.

Bhaskara Rao, Digumarti, Editor (1998). *National Policy on Education: Towards an Enlightened and Humane Society*. New Delhi: Discovery Publishing House. ISBN 81-7141-426-5.

Bhaskara Rao, Digumarti, Editor (1998). *Reforming School Education*. New Delhi: Discovery Publishing House. ISBN 81-7141-403-6.

Bhaskara Rao, Digumarti, Editor (1998). *Teacher Education in India*. New Delhi: Discovery Publishing House. ISBN 81-7141-406-0.

Bhaskara Rao, Digumarti, Editor (1998). *World Summit for Social Development*. New Delhi: Discovery Publishing House. ISBN 81-7141-420-6.

Bhaskara Rao, Digumarti, Editor (1999). *International Encyclopaedia of AIDS*, 11 Volumes. New Delhi: Discovery Publishing House. ISBN 81-7141-522-6 (set).

Vol. 1 *Introduction to HIV/AIDS*. ISBN 81-7141-523-7.

Vol. 2 *HIV/AIDS – Issues and Challenges*, 2 Parts. ISBN 81-7141-524-5.

Vol. 3 *HIV/AIDS—Socio-economic Realities*. ISBN 81-7141-524-3.

Vol. 4 *HIV/AIDS—Law Ethics and Human Rights*, 2 Parts. ISBN 81-7141-526-1.

Vol. 5 *AIDS and NGOs*. ISBN 81-7141-527-X.

Vol. 6 *AIDS and Home Care*. ISBN 81-7141-528-8.

Vol. 7 *STD Case Management*. ISBN 81-7141-529-6.

Vol. 8 *HIV/AIDS Prevention and Care—Teaching Modules for Nurses and Midwives*. ISBN 81-7141-530-X.

Vol. 9 *HIV Prevention Education for Educational Institutions*. ISBN 81-7141-531-8.

Vol. 10 *Instructional Modules for AIDS Education*. ISBN 81-7141-532-6.

Vol. 11 *School Health Education to Prevent AIDS and STD—A Package for Curriculum Planners*. ISBN 81-7141-533-4.

Bhaskara Rao, Digumarti, Editor (2000). *International Encyclopaedia of Human Rights*, 7 Volumes in 13 Parts. New Delhi: Discovery Publishing House. ISBN 81-7141-567-9 (set).

Vol. 1 *International Instruments of Human Rights*, 2 Parts. ISBN 81-7141-569-4.

Vol. 2 *Regional Instruments of Human Rights*. ISBN 81-7141-604-7.

Vol. 3 *Human Rights and the United Nations*, 2 Parts. ISBN 81-7141-605-5.

Vol. 4 *Fact Files of Human Rights*, 3 Parts. ISBN 81-7141-606-3.

Vol. 5 *Study Stories of Human Rights*, 3 Parts. ISBN 81-7141-607-3.

Vol. 6 *International Meetings on Human Rights*, 2 Parts. ISBN 81-714-608-X.

Vol. 7 *Professional Training in Human Rights*. ISBN 81-7141-609-8.

Bhaskara Rao, Digumarti, Editor (2000). *International Encyclopaedia of Science and Technology Education*, 11 Volumes. New Delhi: Discovery Publishing House. ISBN 81-7141-548-2 (set).

Vol. 1 *Science and Technology Education*. ISBN 81-7141-568-7.

Vol. 2 *Science Education in Developing Countries*. ISBN 81-7141-569-9.

Vol. 3 *Organisational Structure of Science*. ISBN 81-7141-570-9.

Vol. 4 *Science Education in Asia and the Pacific*. ISBN 81-7141-571-7.

Vol. 5 *Science and Technology Education For All*. ISBN 81-7141-572-5.

Vol. 6 *Values, Ethics, Talent and Girls in Science and Technology Education*. ISBN 81-7141-573-3.

Vol. 7 *Popularisation of Science and Technology Education*. ISBN 81-7141-574-1.

Vol. 8 *Science, Power and Society*. ISBN 81-7141-575-X.

Vol. 9 *Information Technology*. ISBN 81-7141-576-8.

Vol. 10 *Teacher Training in Science and Technology Education*. ISBN 81-7142-577-6.

Vol. 11 *Teacher Training in Science and Technology: A Curriculum Framework*. ISBN 81-7141-578-4.

Bhaskara Rao, Digumarti, Editor (2000). *Education For All: Achieving the Goal*, 3 Volumes. New Delhi: APH Publishing Corporation. ISBN 81-7648-152-1 (set).

Vol. I *The Global Consensus*. ISBN 81-7648-155-6.

Vol. II *Mid-Decade Review Reports of Regional Seminars*. ISBN 81-7648- 154-8.

Vol. III *Issues and Trends*. ISBN 81-7648-155-6.

Bhaskara Rao, Digumarti, Editor (2001). *Nuclear Materials: Issues and Concerns*, 2 Volumes. New Delhi: Discovery Publishing House. ISBN 81-7141-611-X.

Bhaskara Rao, Digumarti, Editor (2001). *Distance Education in Different Countries*. New Delhi: APH Publishing Corporation. ISBN 81-7648-229-3.

Bhaskara Rao, Digumarti, Editor (2001). *Decentralised Management of Education: Management of Education in Panchayati Raj and Municipal Bodies*. New Delhi: Discovery Publishing House. ISBN 81-7141-617-9.

Bhaskara Rao, Digumarti, Editor (2001). *Electrochemistry for Environmental Protection*. New Delhi: Discovery Publishing House. ISBN 81-7141-619-5.

Bhaskara Rao, Digumarti, Editor (2001). *Global Educational Studies*. New Delhi: Discovery Publishing House. ISBN 81-7141-616-0.

Bhaskara Rao, Digumarti, Editor (2001). *Global Synthesis of Educational Assessment*. New Delhi: Discovery Publishing House. ISBN 81-7141-613-6.

Bhaskara Rao, Digumarti, Editor (2001). *Jomtein Decade of Education*. New Delhi: Discovery Publishing House. ISBN 81-7141-618-7.

Bhaskara Rao, Digumarti, Editor (2001). *World Conference on Education for All*. New Delhi: Discovery Publishing House. ISBN 81-7141-274-9.

Bhaskara Rao, Digumarti, Editor (2001). *World Conference on Higher Education*. New Delhi: Discovery Publishing House. ISBN 81-7141-610-1.

Bhaskara Rao, Digumarti, Editor (2001). *World Conference on Science*. New Delhi: Discovery Publishing House. ISBN 81-7141-612-8.

Bhaskara Rao, Digumarti, Editor (2003). *Inspiring Experiences in Teacher Education*. New Delhi: Discovery Publishing House. ISBN 81-7141-656-X.

Bhaskara Rao, Digumarti, Editor (2003). *International Studies in Education*, 3 Volumes. New Delhi: Discovery Publishing House. ISBN 81-7141-647-0.

Bhaskara Rao, Digumarti, Editor (2003). *Military Conversion: Impact on Science and Technology*. New Delhi: Discovery Publishing House. ISBN 81-7141-578-4.

Bhaskara Rao, Digumarti, Editor (2003). *United Nations Millennium Summit*. New Delhi: Discovery Publishing House. ISBN 81-7141-632-2.

Bhaskara Rao, Digumarti, Editor (2003). *World Assembly on Aging*. New Delhi: Discovery Publishing House. ISBN 81-7141-637-3.

Bhaskara Rao, Digumarti, Editor (2003). *World Conference on Human Rights*. New Delhi: Discovery Publishing House. ISBN 81-7141-661-6.

Bhaskara Rao, Digumarti, Editor (2003). *World Education Forum*. New Delhi: Discovery Publishing House. ISBN 81-7141-639-X.

Bhaskara Rao, Digumarti, Editor (2003). *Education, Employment and Human Resource Development*. New Delhi: Discovery Publishing House. ISBN 81-7141-681-0.

Bhaskara Rao, Digumarti, Editor (2003). *Successful Schooling*. New Delhi: Discovery Publishing House. ISBN 81-7141-677-2.

Bhaskara Rao, Digumarti, Editor (2003). *European Education and Teachers*. New Delhi: Discovery Publishing House. ISBN 81-7141-702-7.

Bhaskara Rao, Digumarti, Editor (2003). *Teachers in a Changing World*. New Delhi: Discovery Publishing House. ISBN 81-7141-694-2.

Bhaskara Rao, Digumarti, Editor (2004). *International Guidelines on Open and Distance Teacher Education*. New Delhi: Discovery Publishing House. ISBN 81-7141-777-9.

Bhaskara Rao, Digumarti, Editor (2004). *Adult Learning in the 21st Century*. New Delhi: Discovery Publishing House. ISBN 81-7141-797-3.

Bhaskara Rao, Digumarti, Editor (2004). *Educational Practices: Research and Recommendations*. New Delhi: Discovery Publishing House. ISBN 81-7141-835-X.

Bhaskara Rao, Digumarti, Editor (2004). *General Secondary Education In the 21st Century*. New Delhi: Discovery Publishing House. ISBN 81-7141-885-6.

Bhaskara Rao, Digumarti, Editor (2004). *International Encyclopaedia of Learning to Live Together*, 4 Volumes. New Delhi: Discovery Publishing House. ISBN 81-7141-848-1.

Vol. 1 *International Conference on Learning to Live Together.*

Vol. 2 *Globalisation and Living Together.*

Vol. 3 *Curriculum for Learning to Live Together.*

Vol. 4 *Science Education for the Contemporary Society.*

Bhaskara Rao, Digumarti, Editor (2004). *Reforming Secondary Education*. New Delhi: Discovery Publishing House. ISBN 81-7141-843-0.

Bhaskara Rao, Digumarti, Editor (2004). *Human Rights Education*. New Delhi: Discovery Publishing House. ISBN 81-7141-882-1.

Bhaskara Rao, Digumarti, Editor (2004). *United Nations Decade for Human Rights Education*. New Delhi: Discovery Publishing House. ISBN 81-7141-887-2.

Bhaskara Rao, Digumarti, Editor (2004). *Technical and Vocational Education and Training in the 21st Century*. New Delhi: Discovery Publishing House. ISBN 81-7141- 984-4.

Bhaskara Rao, Digumarti, Editor (2005). *Encyclopaedia of Education For All*, 5 Volumes. New Delhi: Discovery Publishing House.

Bhaskara Rao, Digumarti and B.S.V. Dutt, Editors (2003). *Education: Programmes and Policies*. New Delhi: APH Publishing Corporation. ISBN 81-7648-470-9.

Bhaskara Rao, Digumarti, C.A.P. Swamy and B.S.V. Dutt (1997). *Self-Evaluation in Student Teaching*. New Delhi: Discovery Publishing House. ISBN 81-7141-374-9.

Bhaskara Rao, Digumarti and D. Naresh Kumar (2004). *School Teacher Effectiveness*. New Delhi: Discovery Publishing House. ISBN 81-7141-782-5.

Bhaskara Rao, Digumarti and D. Sridhar (2002). *Job Satisfaction of School Teachers*. New Delhi: Discovery Publishing House. ISBN 81-7141-652-7.

Bhaskara Rao, Digumarti, C. Sridevi and K. Vijaya (1995). *Achievement in Social Studies*. New Delhi: Discovery Publishing House. ISBN 81-7141-281-5.

Bhaskara Rao, Digumarti and Digumarti Pushpa Latha (1994). *Achievement in Biology*. New Delhi: Discovery Publishing House. ISBN 81-7141-264-5.

Bhaskara Rao, Digumarti and Digumarti Pushpa Latha (1995). *Achievement in English*. New Delhi: Discovery Publishing House. ISBN 81-7141-283-1.

Bhaskara Rao, Digumarti and Digumarti Pushpa Latha (1994). *Achievement in Science*. New Delhi: Discovery Publishing House. ISBN 81-7141-280-70.

Bhaskara Rao, Digumarti and Digumarti Pushpa Latha (1995). *Achievement in Mathematics*. New Delhi: Discovery Publishing House. ISBN 81-7141-278-5.

Bhaskara Rao, Digumarti and Digumarti Pushpa Latha (2004). *Education for Women*. New Delhi: Discovery Publishing House. ISBN 81-7141-873-2.

Bhaskara Rao, Digumarti, Digumarti Pushpa Latha and Digumarthi Harshitha, Editors (2001). *Biological Warfare*. New Delhi: Discovery Publishing House. ISBN 81-7141-597-0.

Bhaskara Rao, Digumarti, Digumarti Pushpa Latha and Digumarthi Harshitha, Editors (2001). *Women as Educators*. New Delhi: Discovery Publishing House. ISBN 81-7141-602-0.

Bhaskara Rao, Digumarti and Digumarthi Harshitha (2004). *Adjustment of Adolescents*. New Delhi: APH Publishing House. ISBN 81-7648-836-8.

Bhaskara Rao, Digumarti and Digumarthi Harshitha, Editors (2001). *Education in India*. New Delhi: APH Publishing House. ISBN 81-7648-207-2.

Bhaskara Rao, Digumarti and Digumarti Pushpa Latha, Editors (1998). *International Encyclopaedia of Women,* 5 Volumes. New Delhi: Discovery Publishing House. ISBN 81-7141-410-9 (set).

Vol. 1 *Status of World's Women.* ISBN 81-7141-494-X.

Vol. 2 *Women, Education and Empowerment.* ISBN 81-7141-498-1.

Vol. 3 *Women Challenges and Advancement.* ISBN 81-7141-497-4.

Vol. 4 *Women and Family Health.* ISBN 81-7141-497-4.

Vol. 5 *Women and International Action.* ISBN 81-7141-498-2.

Bhaskara Rao, Digumarti, Digumarti Pushpa Latha and Digumarthi Harshitha, Editors (2001). *Assessing Learning Achievement.* New Delhi: Discovery Publishing House. ISBN 81-7141-601-2.

Bhaskara Rao, Digumarti, Digumarti Pushpa Latha and Digumarthi Harshitha, Editors (2001). *Energy Security.* New Delhi: Discovery Publishing House. ISBN 81-7141-598-9.

Bhaskara Rao, Digumarti, Digumarthi Harshitha and K.R.S. Sambasiva Rao, Editors (1999). *Advanced Biotechnology.* New Delhi: Discovery Publishing House. ISBN 81-7141-516-4.

Bhaskara Rao, Digumarti and K.R.S. Sambasiva Rao, Editors (1996). *Current Trends in Indian Education.* New Delhi: Discovery Publishing House. ISBN 81-7141-311-0.

Bhaskara Rao, Digumarti and E. Sreekanth Babu (2004). *Educational Interests of School Students.* New Delhi: Discovery Publishing House. ISBN 81-7141-837-6.

Bhaskara Rao, Digumarti and K. Vijaya (1995). *A Text Book Evaluation.* Ambala Cantt: The Associated Publishers.

Bhaskara Rao, Digumarti and M.A. Fayaz (2004). *Problems of Primary School Drop-outs.* New Delhi: Discovery Publishing House. ISBN 81-7141- 834-1.

Bhaskara Rao, Digumarti and N.V.M. Mohana Rao (2002). *Problems of Mentally Handicapped Children.* New Delhi: Discovery Publishing House. ISBN 81-7141-645-4.

Bhaskara Rao, Digumarti and S. Chandra Mohan (2002). *Sports Management*. New Delhi: APH Publishing House. ISBN 81-7648-467-9.

Bhaskara Rao, Digumarti and S.A. Khader (2004). *Problems of Private School Teachers*. New Delhi: Discovery Publishing House. ISBN 81-7141-838-4.

Bhaskara Rao, Digumarti and S.A. Khader (2004). *School Education in India*. New Delhi: Discovery Publishing House. ISBN 81-7141-849-X.

Bhaskara Rao, Digumarti and Sk. Johni Basha (2004). *Teachers' Population Education Awareness*. New Delhi: Discovery Publishing House. ISBN 81-7141-832-5.

Bhaskara Rao, Digumarti, V.V. Rao, V.V. Lakshmi and V.V. Krishna, Editors (1999). *Status and Advancement of Women*. New Delhi: APH Publishing Corporation. ISBN 81-7648-169-6.

Appala Naidu, P.Ch., Author and Digumarti Bhaskara Rao, Editor (2007). *Feedback Methods and Student Performance*. New Delhi: Discovery Publishing House. ISBN 81-8356-284-1.

Babu, P.C., Author and Digumarti Bhaskara Rao, Editor (2004). *Flowers of Wisdom*. New Delhi: Discovery Publishing House. ISBN 81-7141-695-0.

Bujji Babu, K., Author and Digumarti Bhaskara Rao, Editor (2007). *Teaching Aptitude of Primary School Teachers*. New Delhi: Sonali Publications. ISBN 81-8411-083-9.

Amala, P. A. and Anupama, P., Authors and Digumarti Bhaskara Rao, Editor (2004). *History of Education*. New Delhi: Discovery Publishing House. ISBN 81-7141-860-0.

Bhagya Lakshmi, L., Author and Digumarti Bhaskara Rao, Editor (2000). *Reading and Comprehension*. New Delhi: Discovery Publishing House. ISBN 81-7141-543-1.

Bhasha, S.A., Author and Digumarti Bhaskara Rao, Editor (2004). *Methods of Teaching Geography*. New Delhi: Discovery Publishing House. ISBN 81-7141-807-4.

Bhuvaneswara Lakshmi, Gadde, Author and Digumarti Bhaskara Rao, Editor(2000). *Attitude Towards Science*. New Delhi: Discovery Publishing House. ISBN 81-7141-541-6.

Bhuvaneswara Lakshmi, G., Author and Digumarti Bhaskara Rao, Editor (2004). *Methods of Teaching Life Science*. New Delhi: Discovery Publishing House. ISBN 81-7141-804-X.

Bhuvaneswara Lakshmi, G. and K. Subba Rao, Authors and Digumarti Bhaskara Rao, Editor (2004). *Methods of Teaching Biology*. New Delhi: Discovery Publishing House. ISBN 81-7141-914-3.

Chary, K.V.N.B., Author and Digumarti Bhaskara Rao, Editor (2006). *Techniques of Teaching Physics*. New Delhi: Sonali Publications. ISBN 81-8411-046-4.

Chowdary, S.B.J.R. and Naga Raju, Authors and Digumarti Bhaskara Rao, Editor (2004). *Mastery of Teaching Skills*. New Delhi: Discovery Publishing House. ISBN 81-7141-861-9.

Dayakara Reddy, V. and Digumarti Bhaskara Rao, Editors (2006). *Value-Oriented Education*. New Delhi: Discovery Publishing House. ISBN 81-8356-051-2.

Devraj, T.A.S., Author and Digumarti Bhaskara Rao, Editor (1997). *Trace Analysis of Uranium and Thorium*. New Delhi: Discovery Publishing House. ISBN 81-7141-375-7.

Durga Rani, K., Author and Digumarti Bhaskara Rao, Editor (2000). *Educational Aspirations and Scientific Attitudes*. New Delhi: Discovery Publishing House. ISBN 81-7141-555-5.

Dutt, B.S.V. and Digumarti Bhaskara Rao (2001). *Empowering Primary Teachers*. New Delhi: Discovery Publishing House. ISBN 81-7141-615-2.

Dutt, B.S.V., Author and Digumarti Bhaskara Rao, Editor (2004). *Comparative Education*. New Delhi: Discovery Publishing House. ISBN 81-7141-912-7.

Ediger, Marlow and Digumarti Bhaskara Rao (1996). *Science Curriculum*. New Delhi: Discovery Publishing House. ISBN 81-7141-321-8.

Ediger, Marlow and Digumarti Bhaskara Rao (2000). *Teaching Mathematics Successfully.* New Delhi: Discovery Publishing House. ISBN 81-7141-552-0.

Ediger, Marlow and Digumarti Bhaskara Rao (2001). *Teaching Science Successfully.* New Delhi: Discovery Publishing House. ISBN 81-7141-600-4.

Ediger, Marlow and Digumarti Bhaskara Rao (2001). *Teaching Social Studies Successfully.* New Delhi: Discovery Publishing House. ISBN 81-7141-596-2.

Ediger, Marlow and Digumarti Bhaskara Rao (2002). *Philosophy and Curriculum.* New Delhi: Discovery Publishing House. ISBN 81-7141-631-4.

Ediger, Marlow and Digumarti Bhaskara Rao (2002). *Improving School Administration.* New Delhi: Discovery Publishing House. ISBN 81-7141-633-0.

Ediger, Marlow and Digumarti Bhaskara Rao (2002). *Elementary Curriculum.* New Delhi: Discovery Publishing House. ISBN 81-7141-658-6.

Ediger, Marlow and Digumarti Bhaskara Rao (2003). *Language Arts Curriculum.* New Delhi: Discovery Publishing House. ISBN 81-7141-657-8.

Ediger, Marlow and Digumarti Bhaskara Rao (2003). *Psychology and Curriculum.* New Delhi: Discovery Publishing House. ISBN 81-7141-691-8.

Ediger, Marlow and Digumarti Bhaskara Rao (2003). *Teaching Language Arts Successfully.* New Delhi: Discovery Publishing House. ISBN 81-7141-678-0.

Ediger, Marlow and Digumarti Bhaskara Rao (2003). *School Curriculum and Administration.* New Delhi: Discovery Publishing House. ISBN 81-7141-709-4.

Ediger, Marlow and Digumarti Bhaskara Rao (2003). *Teaching Mathematics in Elementary Schools.* New Delhi: Discovery Publishing House. ISBN 81-7141-687-X.

Ediger, Marlow and Digumarti Bhaskara Rao (2003). *Teaching Science in Elementary Schools*. New Delhi: Discovery Publishing House. ISBN 81-7141-698-5.

Ediger, Marlow and Digumarti Bhaskara Rao (2003). *School Curriculum and Administration*. New Delhi: Discovery Publishing House. ISBN 81-7141-709-4.

Ediger, Marlow and Digumarti Bhaskara Rao (2003). *Elementary Curriculum Improvement*. New Delhi: Discovery Publishing House. ISBN 81-7141-740-X.

Ediger, Marlow and Digumarti Bhaskara Rao (2004). *Modern Elementary School*. New Delhi: Discovery Publishing House.

Ediger, Marlow and Digumarti Bhaskara Rao (2004). *School Organisation*. New Delhi: Discovery Publishing House. ISBN 81-7141-843-0.

Ediger, Marlow and Digumarti Bhaskara Rao (2004). *Relevancy in Elementary Curriculum*. New Delhi: Discovery Publishing House. ISBN 81-7141-845-9.

Ediger, Marlow and Digumarti Bhaskara Rao (2005). *Quality School Education*. New Delhi: Discovery Publishing House. ISBN 81-8356-022-9.

Ediger, Marlow and Digumarti Bhaskara Rao (2006). *Successful School Education*. New Delhi: Discovery Publishing House. ISBN 81-8356-054-7.

Ediger, Marlow and Digumarti Bhaskara Rao (2006). *Successful School Administration*. New Delhi: Discovery Publishing House. ISBN 81-8356-046-6.

Ediger, Marlow and Digumarti Bhaskara Rao (2006). *Issues in School Curriculum*. New Delhi: Discovery Publishing House. ISBN 81-8356-052-0.

Ediger, Marlow and Digumarti Bhaskara Rao (2006). *Community College – Curriculum and Teaching*. New Delhi: Discovery Publishing House. ISBN 81-8356-053-9.

Ediger, Marlow and Digumarti Bhaskara Rao (2006). *Administration of Schools*. New Delhi: Discovery Publishing House. ISBN 81-8356-244-2.

Ediger, Marlow and Digumarti Bhaskara Rao (2006). *Reading Curriculum and Instruction*. New Delhi: Discovery Publishing House. ISBN 81-8356-266-3.

Ediger, Marlow and Digumarti Bhaskara Rao (2006). *Curriculum Organisation*. New Delhi: Discovery Publishing House. ISBN 81-8356-205-1.

Ediger, Marlow and Digumarti Bhaskara Rao (2006). *Curriculum of School Subjects*. New Delhi: Discovery Publishing House. ISBN 81-8356-207-8.

Ediger, Marlow, B.S.V. Dutt and Digumarti Bhaskara Rao (2003). *Teaching English Successfully*. New Delhi: Discovery Publishing House. ISBN 81-7141-707-8.

Elizabeth, M.E.S., Author and Digumarti Bhaskara Rao, editor (2004). *Methods of Teaching English*. New Delhi: Discovery Publishing House. ISBN 81-7141-809-0.

Elizabeth, M.E.S., Author and Digumarti Bhaskara Rao, Editor (2004). *Acquisition of English Vocabulary*. New Delhi: Discovery Publishing House. ISBN 81-8356-075-X.

Fatima, Sk. Author and Digumarti Bhaskara Rao, Editor (2007). *Reasoning Ability of School Students*. New Delhi: Discovery Publishing House. ISBN 81-8356-330-9.

Gopala Krishna, M., Author and Digumarti Bhaskara Rao, Editor (2007). *Techniques of Teaching Physical Education*. New Delhi: Sonali Publications. ISBN 81-8411-044-8.

Gopala Krishna, M., Author and Digumarti Bhaskara Rao, Editor (2007). *Techniques of Teaching Education*. New Delhi: Sonali Publications. ISBN 81-8411-062-6.

Harshitha, Digumarthi, Author and Digumarti Bhaskara Rao, Editor (2004). *Methods of Teaching Information Technology*. New Delhi: Discovery Publishing House. ISBN 81-7141-805-8.

Harshitha, Digumarthi, Author and Digumarti Bhaskara Rao, Editor (2007). *Techniques of Teaching Computer Science*. New Delhi: Sonali Publications. ISBN 81-8411-036-7.

Indira Devi, Author and J. Prasanth Kumar and Digumarti Bhaskara Rao, Editors (2004). *Values in Language Text Books*. New Delhi: Discovery Publishing House. ISBN 81-7141-833-3.

Jalaja Kumari, C., Author and Digumarti Bhaskara Rao, Editor (2004). *Methods of Teaching Educational Technology*. New Delhi: Discovery Publishing House. ISBN 81-7141-810-4.

Jalaja Kumari, C., Author and Digumarti Bhaskara Rao, Editor (2007). *Job Satisfaction of Teachers*. New Delhi: Discovery Publishing House. ISBN 81-8356-329-5.

Janardhan Reddy, B., Author and Digumarti Bhaskara Rao, Editor (2006). *Techniques of Teaching Sociology*. New Delhi: Sonali Publications. ISBN 81-8411-042-1.

Jayasree, K., Author and Digumarti Bhaskara Rao, Editor (1999). *Correlates of Socialisation*. New Delhi: Discovery Publishing House. ISBN 81-7141-517-2.

Jayasree, K., Author and Digumarti Bhaskara Rao, Editor (2004). *Methods of Teaching Science*. New Delhi: Discovery Publishing House. ISBN 81-7141-801-5.

John Babu, C., Author and T.J.R. Prasad, G.M. Madhukar and Digumarti Bhaskara Rao, Editors (1996). *Problem Solving in Mathematics*. New Delhi: APH Publishing Corporation. ISBN 81-7648-273-0.

Joseph Raju, B and G.A. Anitha, Authors and Digumarti Bhaskara Rao, Editor (2004). *Population Education*. New Delhi: Sonali Publications. ISBN 81-88836-31-3.

Lalitha, T., Author and K.S. Prabhakaram, D.S.N. Sastry and Digumarti Bhaskara Rao, Editors (2004). *Educational Philosophic Beliefs*. New Delhi: Discovery Publishing House. ISBN 81-7141-765-5.

Krishna, G., Author and Digumarti Bhaskara Rao, Editor (2006). *Techniques of Teaching Physical Education*. New Delhi: Sonali Publications. ISBN 81-8411-044-8.

Kumar Raja, G., Author and Digumarti Bhaskara Rao, Editor (2007). *Principles of Primary School*. New Delhi: Sonali Publications. ISBN 81-8411-054-5.

Lakshmi Kumari, V., Author and Digumarti Bhaskara Rao, Editor (2006). *Techniques of Teaching Home Science*. New Delhi: Sonali Publications. ISBN 81-8411-048-0.

Madhava, K., Author and Digumarti Bhaskara Rao, Editor (2008). *Personality of Adolescent Students*. New Delhi: Discovery Publishing House Pvt. Ltd. ISBN 978-81-8356-262-1.

Madhu Bala, Jampala, Author and Digumarti Bhaskara Rao, Editor (2004). *Methods of Teaching Exceptional Children*. New Delhi: Discovery Publishing House. ISBN 81-7141-802-3.

Madhu Bala, Jampala, Author and Digumarti Bhaskara Rao, Editor (2007). *Adjustment, Problems of Hearing Impaired*. New Delhi: Discovery Publishing House. ISBN 81-7141-831-7.

Marja, Talvi and Digumarti Bhaskara Rao, Editors (1996). *Educational Leadership and Social Changes*. New Delhi: Discovery Publishing House. ISBN 81-7141-320-X.

Mohana Sundari, C., Author and B. Prasad Babu and Digumarti Bhaskara Rao, Editors (2008). *Stress Among Pregnant Women*. New Delhi: Discovery Publishing House Pvt. Ltd. ISBN 978-81-8356-316-1.

Mouni Suvarna Raju, T. J., Author and M.V.R. Raju, B. Prasad Babu and Digumarti Bhaskara Rao, Editors (2008). *Personality and Adjustment of University Hostel Students*. New Delhi: Discovery Publishing House Pvt. Ltd.

Naga Kumari, U., Author and Digumarti Bhaskara Rao, Editor (2008). *Science Process Skills of School Students*. New Delhi: Discovery Publishing House. ISBN 978-81-8356-263-8.

Nageswara Rao, S. and M. Srihari, Authors and Digumarti Bhaskara Rao, Editor (2004). *Guidance and Counselling*. New Delhi: Discovery Publishing House. ISBN 81-7141-840-6.

Nageswara Rao, S., Author and Digumarti Bhaskara Rao, Editor (2006). *Techniques of Teaching Psychology*. New Delhi: Discovery Publishing House. ISBN 81-8411-040-5.

Nageswara Rao, S. and P. Sridhar, Authors and Digumarti Bhaskara Rao, Editor (2004). *Methods and Techniques of Teaching*. New Delhi: Sonali Publications. ISBN 81-88836-33-8.

Nirmala Jyothi, M., Author and Digumarti Bhaskara Rao, Editor (2003). *Non-detention System in School Education*. New Delhi: Discovery Publishing House. ISBN 81-7141-654-3.

Padma Tulasi, G., Author and Digumarti Bhaskara Rao, Editor (2004). *Methods of Teaching Elementary Science*. New Delhi: Discovery Publishing House. ISBN 81-7141-871-6.

Pala Prasada Rao, V., Author and K.N. Rani and D. Bhaskara Rao, Editors (2004). *India Pakistan: Partition Perspectives in Indo-English Novels*. New Delhi: Discovery Publishing House. ISBN 81-7141-871-6.

Pala Prasada Rao, V., Author and D. Bhaskara Rao, Editors (2008). *Functioning of Autonomous Colleges*. New Delhi: Discovery Publishing House. ISBN 978-81-8356-258-4.

Pitchi Reddy, M., Author and Digumarti Bhaskara Rao, Editor (2007). *Techniques of Teaching Social Sciences*. New Delhi: Sonali Publications. ISBN 81-8411-066-X.

Prasad Babu, B., Author and P. Madhu and Digumarti Bhaskara Rao, Editors (2006). *Psychological Adjustment and Well-being*. New Delhi: Discovery Publishing House. ISBN 81-8356-204-3.

Prasad Babu, B., Author and M.V.R. Raju and Digumarti Bhaskara Rao, Editors (2006). *Behavioural Problems of School Children*. New Delhi: Discovery Publishing House. ISBN 81-8356-206-X.

Prabhakaram, K.S., Author and Digumarti Bhaskara Rao, Editors (1998). *Concept Attainment Model in Mathematics Teaching*. New Delhi: Discovery Publishing House. ISBN 81-7141-424-9.

Prasanth Kumar, J., Author and Digumarti Bhaskara Rao, Editor (1998). *Effectiveness of Distance Education System*. New Delhi: Discovery Publishing House. ISBN 81-7141-437-0.

Prasanth Kumar, J., Author and Digumarti Bhaskara Rao, Editor (2004). *Methods of Teaching Civics*. New Delhi: Discovery Publishing House. ISBN 81-7141-806-6.

Prasanth Kumar, J., Author and G. Sundara Rao and Digumarti Bhaskara Rao, Editors (2000). *Open University Student Support Services*. New Delhi: Discovery Publishing House. ISBN 81-7141-550-4.

Raja Kumari, M.A. and D.R.S. Sundari, Authors and Digumarti Bhaskara Rao, Editor (2004). *Special Education*. New Delhi: Discovery Publishing House. ISBN 81-7141-846-5.

Raja Kumari, M.A. and D.R.S. Sundari, Authors and Digumarti Bhaskara Rao, Editor (2004). *Methods of Teaching Educational Psychology*. New Delhi: Discovery Publishing House. ISBN 81-7141-820-1.

Ramatulasamma, K., Author and Digumarti Bhaskara Rao, Editor (2002). *Job Satisfaction of Teacher Educators*. New Delhi: Discovery Publishing House. ISBN 81-7141-655-1.

Rama Krishnaiah, D., Author and Digumarti Bhaskara Rao, Editor (1998). *Job Satisfaction of College Teachers*. New Delhi: Discovery Publishing House. ISBN 81-7141-438-9.

Rama Kumar Ratnam, M.V., Author and Digumarti Bhaskara Rao, Editor (1998). *Dukkha: Suffering in Early Buddhism*. New Delhi: Discovery Publishing House. ISBN 81-7141-653-5.

Rama Krishna Prasad and P. Vide Sagar, Authors and Digumarti Bhaskara Rao, Editor (2004). *Methods of Teaching Physical Education*. New Delhi: Discovery Publishing House. ISBN 81-7141-868-6.

Rama Seshaiah, P. Author and Digumarti Bhaskara Rao, Editor (2004). *Methods of Teaching Home Science*. New Delhi: Discovery Publishing House. ISBN 81-7141-916-X.

Rama Swamy, K., Author and Digumarti Bhaskara Rao, Editor (2007). *Techniques of Teaching Environmental Science*. New Delhi: Sonali Publications. ISBN 81-8411-035-9.

Ramesh, A.R., Author and Digumarti Bhaskara Rao, Editor (2006). *Techniques of Teaching Commerce*. New Delhi: Sonali Publications. ISBN 81-8411-043-X.

Ramesh, Ghanta and Digumarti Bhaskara Rao, Editors (1998). *Environmental Education: Problems and Prospects*. New Delhi: Discovery Publishing House. ISBN 81-7141-423-0.

Ranga Rao, B., Author and Digumarti Bhaskara Rao, Editor (2007). *Techniques of Teaching Economics*. New Delhi: Sonali Publications. ISBN 81-8411-056-1.

Ranga Rao, R., Author and Digumarti Bhaskara Rao, Editor (2004). *Methods of Teacher Teaching*. New Delhi: Discovery Publishing House. ISBN 81-7141-812-0.

Rajeswari, S.M., Author and T. Santhanam, B. Prasad Babu and Digumarti Bhaskara Rao, Editors (2008). *Stress Among Women Teachers Working with Normal and Special Children*. New Delhi: Discovery Publishing House.

Rani, S.S., Author and Digumarti Bhaskara Rao, Editor (2006). *Techniques of Teaching Botany*. New Delhi: Sonali Publications. ISBN 81-8411-037-5.

Rathaiah, Lavu and Digumarti Bhaskara Rao, Editors (1996), *International Innovations in Education*. New Delhi: Discovery Publishing House. ISBN 81-7141-359-5.

Rathaiah, Lavu and Digumarti Bhaskara Rao (1997). *Achievement Correlates*. New Delhi: Discovery Publishing House. ISBN 81-7141-385-4.

Ravi Krishna, M., Author and Digumarti Bhaskara Rao, Editor (2004). *Examination System*. New Delhi: Discovery Publishing House. ISBN 81-7141-824-4.

Ravi Kumar, M., Author and Digumarti Bhaskara Rao, Editor (2004). *Methods of Teaching Computer Science*. New Delhi: Discovery Publishing House. ISBN 81-7141-823-6.

Rudramamba, B., Author and Digumarti Bhaskara Rao, Editor (2003). *Problems of Teaching*. New Delhi: APH Publishing Corporation. ISBN 81-7648-462-8.

Rudramamba, B. and V. Lakshmi Kumari, Authors and Digumarti Bhaskara Rao, Editor (2004). *Methods of Teaching Economics*. New Delhi: Discovery Publishing House. ISBN 81-7141-900-3.

Sambasiva Rao, P., Author and Digumarti Bhaskara Rao, Editor (2007). *Techniques of Teaching Psychology*. New Delhi: Sonali Publications. ISBN 81-8411-040-5.

Sanjeeva Rao, P.C., Author and Digumarti Bhaskara Rao, Editor (1996). *A Text Book of Geology*. New Delhi: Discovery Publishing House. ISBN 81-7141-313-7.

Santhanam, T., B. Prasad Babu and S. Sugandhi, Authors and Digumarti Bhaskara Rao, Editor (2008). *Learning Disabilities and Remedial Programmes*. New Delhi: Discovery Publishing House. ISBN 978-81-8356-257-7.

Santhanam, T., B. Prasad Babu and S. Sugandhi, authors and Digumarti Bhaskara Rao, Editor (2007). *Children with Learning Disabilities*. New Delhi: Sonali Publications. ISBN 81-8411-077-4.

Sarala, M.M.O., Author and Digumarti Bhaskara Rao, Editor (2006). *Techniques of Teaching English*. New Delhi: Sonali Publications. ISBN 81-8411-047-2.

Satya Narayana, G., Author and Digumarti Bhaskara Rao, Editor (2008). *Attitude towards Social Studies and Achievement in Social Studies*. New Delhi: Discovery Publishing House Pvt. Ltd. ISBN 978-81-8356-261-4.

Satya Narayana, V., Author and Digumarti Bhaskara Rao, Editor (2001). *Physical Education, Social Attitudes and Leadership Qualities*. New Delhi: Discovery Publishing House. ISBN 81-7141-593-8.

Satya Narayana, P.V.V. and G. Krishna, Authors and Digumarti Bhaskara Rao, Editor (2004). *Curriculum Development and Management*. New Delhi: Discovery Publishing House. ISBN 81-7141-813-9.

Shamsuddin, Sk. and V. Dayakara Reddy, Authors and Digumarti Bhaskara Rao, Editor (2007). *Academic Achievement and Values*. New Delhi: Discovery Publishing House.

Singh, Y.C., Author and Digumarti Bhaskara Rao, Editor (2006). *Techniques of Teaching Science*. New Delhi: Sonali Publications. ISBN 81-8411-041-3.

Sirisha Rani, S., Author and Digumarti Bhaskara Rao, Editor (2007). *Techniques of Teaching Botany*. New Delhi: Sonali Publications. ISBN 81-8411-037-5.

Sivaratnam Reddy, M., Author and Digumarti Bhaskara Rao, Editor (2004). *Creativity in College Students*. New Delhi: Discovery Publishing House. ISBN 81-7141-697-7.

Siva Lakshmi, G.V. and G.L. Subbaiah, Authors and Digumarti Bhaskara Rao, Editor (2004). *Methods of Teaching Environmental Science*. New Delhi: Discovery Publishing House. ISBN 81-7141-839-2.

Srinivas, G., Author and Digumarti Bhaskara Rao, Editor (2007). *Anxiety of Prospective Teachers*. New Delhi: Discovery Publishing House.

Srinivas, M. and I. Prasada Rao, Authors and Digumarti Bhaskara Rao, Editor (2004). *Methods of Teaching History*. New Delhi: Discovery Publishing House. ISBN 81-7141-803-1.

Srinivas Rao, P., Author and Digumarti Bhaskara Rao, Editor (2007). *Principles of Secondary School*. New Delhi: Sonali Publications. ISBN 81-8411-058-8.

Srinivasulu Reddy, M. and K.R.S. Sambasiva Rao, Authors and Digumarti Bhaskara Rao, Editor (1999). *A Text Book of Aquaculture*. New Delhi: Discovery Publishing House. ISBN 81-7141-482-6.

Srinivasa Rao, Mandalapu, Author and Digumarti Bhaskara Rao, Editor (2003). *Achievement Motivation and Achievement in Mathematics*. New Delhi: Discovery Publishing House. ISBN 81-7141-674-8.

Srihari, M., Author and Digumarti Bhaskara Rao, Editor (2003). *Values of Prospective Teachers*. New Delhi: Discovery Publishing House. ISBN 81-8356-328-7.

Subba Rao, K., Author and Digumarti Bhaskara Rao, Editor (2007). *School Education Policy*. New Delhi: Discovery Publishing House. ISBN 81-8356-285-X.

Subba Rao, K., Author and Digumarti Bhaskara Rao, Editor (2007). *Education Planning*. New Delhi: Sonali Publications. ISBN 81-8411-053-7.

Sudhakar Reddy, Y., Author and Digumarti Bhaskara Rao, Editor (2003). *Creativity in Adolescents*. New Delhi: Discovery Publishing House. ISBN 81-7141-659-4.

Sunil Kumar, K. and K. Rama Krishana, Authors and Digumarti Bhaskara Rao, Editor (2004). *Methods of Teaching Chemistry*. New Delhi: Discovery Publishing House. ISBN 81-7141-913-5.

Suneetha, G., Author and Digumarti Bhaskara Rao, Editor (2004). *Environmental Awareness of School Students*. New Delhi: Sonali Publications. ISBN 81-8411-085-5.

Sunita, E. and R. Sambasiva Rao, Authors and Digumarti Bhaskara Rao, Editor (2004). *Methods of Teaching Mathematics*. New Delhi: Discovery Publishing House. ISBN 81-7141-915-1.

Surya Madhava, I., Author and Digumarti Bhaskara Rao, Editor (2006). *Techniques of Teaching Geography*. New Delhi: Sonali Publications. ISBN 81-8411-034-0.

Surya Madhava, I., Author and Digumarti Bhaskara Rao, Editor (2007). *Techniques of Teaching Political Science*. New Delhi: Sonali Publications. ISBN 81-8411-061-8.

Swamy, K.R., Author and Digumarti Bhaskara Rao, Editor (2006). *Techniques of Teaching Environmental Science*. New Delhi: Sonali Publications. ISBN 81-8411-035-9.

Swarna Jyothi, K., Author and Digumarti Bhaskara Rao, Editor (2007). *Educational Research*. New Delhi: Sonali Publications. ISBN 81-8411-063-4.

Swarna Latha, C.D., and Digumarti Bhaskara Rao, Editors (2006). *Encyclopaedia of Biotechnology*, 5 Volumes. New Delhi: Discovery Publishing House. ISBN 81-8356-168-3. (set).

Swarupa Rani, T. and J.R. Priyadarshini, Authors and Digumarti Bhaskara Rao, Editor (2004). *Educational Measurement and Evaluation*. New Delhi: Discovery Publishing House. ISBN 81-7141-859-7.

Vanaja, M., Author and Digumarti Bhaskara Rao, Editor (1999). *Inquiry Training Model*. New Delhi: Discovery Publishing House. ISBN 81-7141-515-6.

Vanaja, M., Author and Digumarti Bhaskara Rao, Editor (2004). *Methods of Teaching Physics*. New Delhi: Discovery Publishing House. ISBN 81-7141-867-8.

Valeri V. Koustiouk, Author and Digumarti Bhaskara Rao, Editor (2002). *A Text Book of Cryogenics*. New Delhi: Discovery Publishing House. ISBN 81-7141-642-X.

Vamsi Krishna, V., Author and Digumarti Bhaskara Rao, Editor (2004). *School Psychology*. New Delhi: Discovery Publishing House. ISBN 81-7141-880-5.

Veena Kumari, Balusu and Digumarti Bhaskara Rao (1996). *Operation Black Board*. New Delhi: APH Publishing Corporation. ISBN 81-7024-711-X.

Veena Kumari, Balusu, Author and Digumarti Bhaskara Rao, Editor (2004). *Methods of Teaching Social Studies*. New Delhi: Discovery Publishing House. ISBN 81-7141-899-6.

Veena Kumari, Balusu, Author and Digumarti Bhaskara Rao, Editor (2000). *Psycho-Social Correlates of Achievement*. New Delhi: Discovery Publishing House. ISBN 81-7141-547-4.

Venkata Rao, B., Author and Digumarti Bhaskara Rao, Editor (2007). *Techniques of Teaching Chemistry*. New Delhi: Sonali Publications. ISBN 81-8411-057-X.

Venkata Rao, P. and Digumarti Bhaskara Rao (1989). *A Text Book of Zoology – Junior Intermediate*. Guntur: Vignan Publishers.

Venkata Rao, P. and Digumarti Bhaskara Rao (1989). *A Text Book of Zoology – Senior Intermediate*. Guntur: Vignan Publishers.

Venkateswara Rao, V., Author and Digumarti Bhaskara Rao, Editor (2004). *Problems of Education*. New Delhi: Discovery Publishing House. ISBN 81-7141-841-4.

Venkateswara Rao, V., V. Vijaya Lakshmi and V. Vamsi Krishna, Authors and Digumarti Bhaskara Rao, Editor (2004). *Education For All*. New Delhi: Sonali Publications. ISBN 81-88836-30-3.

Venkateswara Rao, V., V. Vijaya Lakshmi and V. Vamsi Krishna, Authors and Digumarti Bhaskara Rao, Editor (2004). *Education in India*. New Delhi: Sonali Publications. ISBN 81-88836-858-9.

Venkateswara Reddy, L. and Narayana, M. L., Authors and Digumarti Bhaskara Rao, Editor (2004). *Education for Dalits*. New Delhi: Discovery Publishing House. ISBN 81-7141-872-4.

Venkateswara Reddy, L. and Narayana, M. L, Authors and Digumarti Bhaskara Rao, Editor (2004). *Methods of Teaching Rural Sociology*. New Delhi: Discovery Publishing House. ISBN 81-7141-811-2.

Venkateswarlu, K. and S.J. Basha, Authors and Digumarti Bhaskara Rao, Editor (2004). *Methods of Teaching Commerce*. New Delhi: Discovery Publishing House. ISBN 81-7141-808-2.

Venugopala Rao, K., Author and Digumarti Bhaskara Rao, Editor (2000). *Teacher Morale in Secondary Schools*. New Delhi: Discovery Publishing House. ISBN 81-7141-551-2.

Venugopala Rao, K., Author and Digumarti Bhaskara Rao, Editor (2007). *Techniques of Teaching history*. New Delhi: Sonali Publications. ISBN 81-8411-059-6.

Vidya, C., Author and Digumarti Bhaskara Rao, Editor (1996). *A Text Book of Nutrition*. New Delhi: Discovery Publishing House. ISBN 81-7141-309-9.

Vimala, T.D., B. Prasad Babu and Digumarti Bhaskara Rao, Editors (2007). *Stress, Coping and Management*. New Delhi: Sonali Publications. ISBN 81-8411-086-3.

Vijaya Bharathi, D., Author and Digumarti Bhaskara Rao, Editor (2000). *Educational Philosophies of Swami Vivekananda and John Dewey*. New Delhi: APH Publishing House. ISBN 81-7648-309-9.

Vijaya Bharathi, D., Author and Digumarti Bhaskara Rao, Editor (2005). *Educational Philosophy of John Dewey*. New Delhi: Discovery Publishing House. ISBN 81-8356-024-5.

Vijaya Bharathi, D., Author and Digumarti Bhaskara Rao, Editor (2005). *Educational Philosophy of Swami Vivekananda*. New Delhi: Discovery Publishing House. ISBN 81-8356-023-7.

Vijaya Lakshmi, D., Author and Digumarti Bhaskara Rao, Editor (2004) *Basic Education*. New Delhi: Discovery Publishing House. ISBN 81-7141-881-3.

Vijaya Lakshmi, V., Author and Digumarti Bhaskara Rao, Editor (2006). *Techniques of Teaching Music*. New Delhi: Sonali Publications. ISBN 81-8411-038-3.

Vijaya Kumar, S.J., Author and Digumarti Bhaskara Rao, Editor (2006). *Techniques of Teaching Mathematics*. New Delhi: Sonali Publications. ISBN 81-8411-039-1.

Visalakshi, V., Author and Digumarti Bhaskara Rao, Editor (2006). *Techniques of Teaching Biology*. New Delhi: Sonali Publications. ISBN 81-8411-045-6.

Visalakshi, V., Author and Digumarti Bhaskara Rao, Editor (2007). *Techniques of Teaching Zoology*. New Delhi: Sonali Publications. ISBN 81-8411-055-3.

Bhaskara Rao, Digumarti (1986). *Dhrushya Sravana Bodhanapakaranalu* (Audio-visual Teaching Aids). Guntur: Nagarjuna Publishers.

Bhaskara Rao, Digumarti (1993). *Jeevasashtra Bodhana* (Teaching of Biology). Guntur: Nagarjuna Publishers.

Bhaskara Rao, Digumarti (1995). *Vignanasasthra Bodhana* (Teaching of Science) Guntur: Nagarjuna Publishers.

Bhaskara Rao, Digumarti (1997). *Vidya Manovignana Sastram* (Educational Psychology). Guntur: Creative Press.

Bhaskara Rao, Digumarti (1998). *DSC Study Material*. Guntur: Nagarjuna Publishers.

Bhaskara Rao, Digumarti (1998). *Upadhyayudu Vidya*. (Teacher and Education) Guntur: Nagarjuna Publishers.

Bhaskara Rao, Digumarti (1998). *Vidya Drukpadalu* (Perspectives of Education). Guntur: Nagarjuna Publishers.

Bhaskara Rao, Digumarti (1999). *EdCET Teaching Aptitude*. Guntur: Nagarjuna Publishers.

Bhaskara Rao, Digumarti (2001). *Bharata Samajamulo Upadyayudu Vidhya* (Teacher and Education in Emerging Indian Society). Guntur: Sri Nagarjuna Publishers.

Bhaskara Rao, Digumarti (2001). *Bhoutika Sastra Bodhana Padhatulu* (Methods of Teaching Physical Science). Guntur: Sri Nagarjuna Publishers.

Bhaskara Rao, Digumarti (2001). *Jeeva Sastra Bodhana Padhatulu* (Methods of Teaching Biology).Guntur: Sri Nagarjuna Publishers.

Bhaskara Rao, Digumarti (2001). *Vidya Manovignana Sastram* (Educational Psychology). Guntur: Sri Nagarjuna Publishers.

Bhaskara Rao, Digumarti (2003). *Patasala Yajamanyam/Paripalana* (School Management and Administration). Guntur: Sri Nagarjuna Publishers.

Gopala Krishna, G., A. Rama Krishna, K. Subba Rao and Bhaskara Rao, Digumarti (2004). *Jeevasashtra Bodhana Padhatulu* (Methods of Teaching of Biological Science). Guntur: Sri Nagarjuna Publishers.

Krishna Murthy, V., K.S. Sudheer Reddy and Digumarti Bhaskara Rao (2004). *Vidya Manovignana Sastra Adharalu* (Foundations of Educational Psychology). Guntur: Sri Nagarjuna Publishers.

Lalini, V., V. Dayakara Reddy, M. Srihari and Digumarti Bhaskara Rao (2004). *Vidya Adharalu* (Foundations of Education). Guntur: Sri Nagarjuna Publishers.

Subba Rao, K.P., P. Ayodhya and Digumarti Bhaskara Rao (2004). *Patasala Yajamanyam – Vidhya Vyavasthalu* (School Management and Systems of Education). Guntur: Sri Nagarjuna Publishers.

Sudhakar, V., B. Ravindra Babu, D.S. Kumar and Digumarti Bhaskara Rao (2004). *Vidya Sanketika Sastram—Computer Vidhya* (Educational Technology and Computer Education). Guntur: Sri Nagarjuna Publishers.

Index

G

H

I

J

K

L

M

N

O

P

Q

R

S

T

V

W

Z

❑❑❑